I0605505

The Queen You Thought You Knew

David Fohrman

THE QUEEN YOU THOUGHT YOU KNEW

UNMASKING ESTHER'S HIDDEN STORY

Aleph Beta Press
Maggid Books

The Queen You Thought You Knew
Second Edition, 2024

Maggid Books
An imprint of Koren Publishers Jerusalem Ltd.

POB 8531, New Milford, CT 06776-8531, USA
& POB 4044, Jerusalem 9104001, Israel
www.maggidbooks.com

Aleph Beta Press
info@alephbeta.org
www.alephbeta.org

The publication of this book was made possible
through the generous support of *The Jewish Book Trust.*

ISBN 978-1 59264-616-6, *hardcover*

Printed and bound in the United States

Contents

Acknowledgments

Every once in a while, one comes to a fork in the road of life and senses that the choice he makes at that moment will guide the direction he takes for years. One such moment took place for me two decades ago when, after a class I gave on Genesis at Johns Hopkins University, LeRoy Hoffberger and his wife, Rebecca, lingered for a fascinating extended discussion on the themes we had been talking about in class. In subsequent conversations on other evenings in a Johns Hopkins parking lot, and later in their home, we began to forge a bond that would flourish over the years. LeRoy and Rebecca cared deeply about the underlying meaning of biblical stories, and more generally, about how knowledge of Torah can and should inform one's life. In short order, LeRoy had created the Hoffberger Foundation for Torah Studies, which has ardently supported my work since then. Teaching biblical themes had always been a passion of mine, but I never thought I'd be fortunate enough to devote my professional life to that dream. LeRoy began to make that dream a reality for me. Through his efforts, a conversation in a parking lot has blossomed into countless classes – and now, several books. Along the way, he has become a close friend, a devoted student, a valued mentor, and an unfailing source of guidance. I am deeply privileged to call him a partner in my life's work.

In recent years, others have joined the effort to take the methodology and material that I've developed thus far and project it further into the world at large. These devoted souls have spearheaded the further development of LeRoy Hoffberger's vision, creating the newly-formed Hoffberger Institute for Text Study.

The mission of this institute is to help make biblical text come alive, to help enable students across the globe to build a living, vibrant relationship with these ancient, seemingly inaccessible texts. To this end, it supports the publication of books and curriculum materials, video presentations, and teacher development. I am grateful to the founding members of this institute who, in the process of helping to make this dream take shape, have also become my close friends: Jeffrey Haskell, Yoni Kahan, Josh Mallin, Glen and Ruth Miller, David Pollack, Robby Rothenberg, Joel Rothman, Kuty Shalev, Stephen Wagner, and Adrian Weller. Many participated in the process of bringing this book from the realm of vision into reality. Chief among them are Andrew and Terri Herenstein, who have graciously become patrons of this volume. Terri participated actively in a Monday morning class where I first formulated the thoughts that became the core of this book, and has been in on the development of these ideas from the very beginning. Terri and Andrew's enthusiasm, generous support, friendship, and wise counsel all mean a great deal to me.

I am grateful to Stephen and Tamara Wagner, whose efforts and generosity will place this book and others in the hands of scores of students. They have undertaken to launch the institute's School Enrichment Program – an ambitious effort that seeks to place books we publish, free of charge, in the hands of students across the country. I am grateful for their vision and generosity. Since my arrival in Woodmere, Steve has been a close friend, a trusted advisor, and an insightful collaborator in the world of ideas. I value deeply all he does to nurture my efforts. I am grateful to Maggid Books for their professionalism in producing this edition of the book, as well as to OU Press and Aleph Beta, who published earlier editions.

I want to thank my good friend Kuty Shalev, founder and president of the board of Aleph Beta, who has devoted himself to the goals of the institute and the production of this book with single-minded zeal. He has freely given of his time and expertise to this cause. Kuty has taken charge of the operational side of the institute with a passion that has proved contagious. He skillfully shepherded the production of this book in a precipitously short time frame. Kuty was assisted in this by Daniel Weisblum, who managed typesetting and logistical coordination with talent and good cheer. Carol Wise capably edited the manuscript, and Daniel Yarmish and Naomi Gross proofread it. The cover design was conceived and executed by Marcel Sendrea. A hearty thank-you to Cory Rockliff for editing and typesetting the second edition.

I'd also like to thank a number of people who devoted their time to read the manuscript, give feedback, and make valuable comments and suggestions. They include Searle Mitnick, LeRoy Hoffberger, Stephen Wagner, Barry Waldman, Tzvi Nachman, David Pollack, Naomi Gross, Daniel Yarmish, Danielle Bloom, David Kirshtein, Shlomo Horowitz, and Meyer Stender. I am grateful to each and every one.

Recently, I've been privileged to serve as resident scholar at the Young Israel of Woodmere, and in that role I've been delivering a weekly lecture series at the Young Israel's Nusach Sefard Minyan. That lecture has been a proving ground for new ideas, and was an arena in which I pioneered many of the approaches and themes for this book. I'd like to thank the attendees of those lectures for their vigorous participation, questions, and feedback; they have contributed substantially to the development of the pages that follow.

In this connection, I'd also like to thank Rabbi Herschel Billet, senior rabbi at the Young Israel of Woodmere, for his guidance, counsel, and friendship over the years, and for making the Young Israel such a welcoming home for the work that I do. It is an honor to be associated with him and with the rest of the Young Israel's outstanding rabbinic staff. My thanks go, as well, to Shlomo Zuller, president of the congregation, who, along with Shaul Shwalb and Steven Wagner, was instrumental in bringing the Nusach Sefard Minyan into being, and has attentively nurtured its development.

Before an author writes a book, he needs to actually have something to say. In that spirit, I want to acknowledge those who, over the years, helped shape my way of thinking and guide my development as a student of Torah.

The person who perhaps most profoundly influenced my life and way of thinking was my late father, Moshe Fohrman, *zt"l.* He died before I became a bar mitzvah, but in those early years, he taught me much of what I know about what makes life worthwhile, and how to practice the art of living in a meaningful way. Despite the passage of years, he remains a vivid role model for me, and I hope that he would regard this book as a worthy expression of his legacy.

I spent many years studying at the Ner Israel Rabbinical College and feel honored to count the *rosh yeshiva* of that institution, the late Rabbi Yaakov Weinberg, *zt"l,* as a mentor. Other faculty members at Ner Israel – including Rabbis Tzvi Berkowitz, Moshe Eisenmann, Nachum Lansky, and Ezra Neuberger – introduced new vistas of thinking to me. The late Rabbi Naftoli Neuberger, *zt"l,* was a defining figure in my life, in many and varied ways. He offered abundant guidance and love and was truly like a second father to me.

I am grateful for the support of a loving family. Throughout the years, my mother, Mrs. Nechama Wolfson, has been an emotional bulwark for me. When she married my stepfather, Mr. Zev Wolfson, she brought into my life a man who has come to share her intense interest in my welfare and development. I am proud to have become part of his family.

My children, besides being terrific kids, have also helped in this journey. I want to acknowledge my son, Moshe, who read through the manuscript and contributed incisive and subtle changes. He gave the work no special quarter due to the incidental fact that it was written by his father – and in the end, the manuscript is sharper for it. The occasional flashes of concision in the book owe something to Shalva, whose distaste for wordiness is palpable. Avigail provided careful analysis of the book's ending and helped refine other parts as well. Shoshana helped eliminate repetitious passages and remarked that she couldn't put the book down – words any father would be touched by. And my younger kids? Well, having them around while writing certainly made my days brighter.

My wife is my biggest fan – and is also an incisive critic. When I asked her to go over parts of the work with me, her sharp instincts won out over her emotional allegiances – and for this I am grateful, for every part she touched was enriched thereby. More generally, on car rides and on walks, she parried the ideas in the book back and forth with me and helped me sharpen them. Her loving attention and belief in my work has given me the strength and emotional sustenance to go forward in life. I am privileged to have her as my life's partner, and hope and pray we shall celebrate many more milestones together.

Introduction

The Book of Esther can easily masquerade as a tale for children. There's a villain who is out to hang Mordecai and murder his countrymen, a king who enjoys drinking and seems a bit naïve, and a beautiful and noble queen. There are assassins, palace intrigue, and a climactic battle scene to boot. There's even a happy ending. What more could you ask for in a good children's story?

The holiday associated with the book can seem childish too. Purim is celebrated with costumes, carnivals, and abundant merriment. Our kids dress up as Esther, Mordecai, Haman, and Ahasuerus. They wear plastic hats and carry cellophane scepters. Purim is the great holiday of make-believe.

All this make-believe, though, can have unintended consequences. Chief among them is the disheartening fact that we are likely to retain childlike views of Purim and the Book of Esther long after we've become adults. If you first learned about Esther and Haman when you were six years old, you may well still see them the same way now. Our view of Mordecai and Esther and their struggle can easily remain as flat as the face paint we use to impersonate these people in costume.

There is another Purim story out there, a richer, deeper narrative – more suited, perhaps, to the eyes of an adult than to those of a child. But in order to see that story, we need to let go mentally of everything we thought we knew about the Book of Esther and read her tale anew, as if for the first time. We need to allow ourselves to be surprised by it.

GETTING COMFORTABLE WITH DISSONANCE

You don't have to be a rocket scientist to see the surprises. You just have to read with open eyes. Remember that game you sometimes played when you were young, "What's Wrong with This Picture"? There would be a nice forest scene complete with flora, fauna, sky, sun, and clouds. At first, everything seemed normal. But if you looked closely, you would find that little things were askew. There was a toaster plugged into a tree. Or a shadow was out of alignment with the sun. One by one, you'd have to collect the problems until you were satisfied that you had found them all.

In this book, we are going to read the Book of Esther as if we were playing that game. Everything seems simple and straightforward. But then you start to notice the toasters plugged into the trees. There are irrelevant asides, useless digressions, and characters that seem to do the silliest things. The picture that seemed so simple, so innocent, and so childlike suddenly seems vaguely unnerving and out of kilter. The sun is out of alignment with the shadows.

These surprises are clues. They are guideposts that illuminate a deeper story, one that lies just beneath the surface of the text. If we piece together enough of these clues, we will end up glimpsing the hidden face of the Book of Esther, a three-dimensional story of stark emotional power and spiritual import, a story that begins in earnest just when most of us think the narrative is virtually over. This hidden narrative tells not just of Esther's battle against an external villain in the form of Haman, but of her simultaneous struggle against an internal threat, a faceless, subtle menace that had haunted the Jewish people for centuries. It is a story with roots in the dawn of Jewish history, but it is equally fresh and relevant in our own time. It is a story that reveals itself gradually to the patient reader willing to ask questions and notice anomalies.

When we were young, we built with little colored blocks; as we matured, so did our ideas about architecture. When we were young, we counted with our fingers; as we matured, so did our ideas about mathematics. Well, when we were young, we also learned about the Bible. But did we ever allow our ideas to mature, or are we stuck with the same six-year-old view we had when we were playing with colored blocks and counting on our fingers?

Taking note of the toasters in the trees can be thrilling, if at times somewhat bewildering. But if we accept the challenge and read with open eyes, we may find ourselves enchanted anew by the drama of the queen we thought we knew. Indeed, we shall find her world resplendent with meaning, if only we are willing to enter it.

Part I

The Megilla's Forgotten Ending

Chapter One

Some Opening Questions

WHY DOES THE MEGILLA LAST SO LONG?

The crowd is restless. It is an hour and a half after sundown on Purim night. People have been fasting all day long. For the last thirty minutes or so, the crowd has been listening to the Megilla being read aloud. They have heard about how Ahasuerus, king of Persia, ruled the world; how Vashti, his first wife, met her demise; and about the beauty contest in which Esther, a secret Jew, was chosen queen. They have heard how Mordecai the Jew incited the rage of Haman, and how Haman plotted to eradicate the Jewish people in revenge. They've heard how, in the end, Esther foiled Haman's plot.

The story has reached its climax: Haman is dead. Mordecai and Esther are rewarded. The good guys have won; the bad guys have met with their sorry fate. It looks like the happy ending has arrived. You'd think the crowd would be getting ready to leave the synagogue and break their fast.

But they're not, because for some reason, the Megilla isn't over. There are still another three chapters to go.

Strangely, the Book of Esther seems to overstay its welcome; it seems to last fifteen minutes too long. Why are there three chapters left after the Jews have already been saved and Haman has been killed? What, really, is there left to say?

Look at what happens in these last three chapters: Mordecai issues some decrees. Horsemen run here; horsemen run there. The Jews successfully defend themselves on the day they were supposed to be destroyed. A long series of proclamations is issued in which the events are memorialized in a holiday to be called "Purim." Why do we need to hear about all of this in such detail? Why not summarize it in just a few sentences, something like: *And after Haman was hanged, the Jews killed their enemies; Mordecai and Esther proclaimed that the victory be memorialized forevermore as "Purim," and everyone lived happily ever after.*

There, that seems simple enough – and it's just three sentences long. Why does it take three chapters to say *that*? Doesn't such a long-winded ending detract from the dramatic power of the story?

In the pages that follow, we will try to answer this question and arrive at an understanding of the events that occur in the often-overlooked final three chapters of the Book of Esther. By the end, we will see that these chapters are vitally important to the story, that indeed, what appears to be the story's climax is not its climax, and in the apparently humdrum details of the last three chapters lies a riveting conclusion to a hidden story. Unearthing this hidden story and its various implications will be the central quest of this book.

A SEARCH FOR QUESTIONS

To discern the hidden face of the Megilla, we must first discover what is startling about its ordinary face, the story we have known and loved so well since childhood. Let's begin, then, by taking a step back and trying to ask the questions any intelligent adult would ask were he or she reading the Megilla – or celebrating Purim, for that matter – for the very first time. Here are a few of those questions that have occurred to me over the years. I wonder if they've ever bothered you too.

TOKAREV DAY

One of the strangest aspects of the Book of Esther, or "the Megilla," as we shall sometimes call it, is the name that it gives to the holiday that will enshrine the events of which it tells. According to the Megilla, this holiday is to be named Purim – a name that persists to this day – after the lots (*pur*) that Haman cast to determine the day upon which he and his minions would murder all the Jews.

Now, imagine you were living at the time when the events of the Megilla took place. The Jews had managed to avoid what seemed like certain destruction, and a holiday was to be freshly minted to commemorate these miraculous events. All that remained was to come up with a name for it. You, as it happens, are one of the elders elected to the naming committee for the prospective holiday. You brainstorm with your colleagues and come up with a few possible names. Some people in the room have suggested "Esther Day" or "Mordecai Day." Others thought it might be called "Salvation Day" or even "Victory in Persia Day." But now imagine that some fellow in the back of the room comes up with a novel suggestion: "Why don't we call it Purim?" he says. Everyone turns around and looks. Finally, someone asks, "Why call it that?"

"Well," the fellow replies, "you know, when Haman was trying to kill us, he cast the *pur* (lots) to select a day on which he would kill us all. So let's call it after that whole 'lots' thing. Let's call the holiday Purim, for the 'lots.'" What would you think of this fellow's suggestion? Is this a really terrific name for the holiday? It doesn't take all that much reflection to raise some objections.

First, why would you name a holiday after the device your nemesis used to try to kill you? Why give the day to him? It seems bizarre, and perhaps the only reason we don't immediately realize just how bizarre it seems is that this is what we ourselves have called the holiday since we were children. But to escape that effect, imagine a similar phenomenon with respect to another holiday – say, Yom HaAtzma'ut, Israel's Day of Independence.

Imagine it is 1948; Israel has just proclaimed its statehood and managed to ward off several invading Arab armies. The question comes up; people will want to celebrate this moment year after year. What should we name the day? Someone in the back of the room raises his hand and says, "Let's call it Tokarev Day." "Why Tokarev Day?" everyone asks. "Well," he continues, "when the Arabs tried to kill us all, their weapon of choice was the Russian-made, self-loading Tokarev rifle. Thank God, we were saved. So let's call it Tokarev Day!" And everyone applauds and decides that this is a wonderful name for the new holiday. That's roughly what seems to have happened with Purim. Why name the day after the instrument of our enemy? It's not *his* holiday; it's ours!

CHANCE, FATE, AND PROVIDENCE

In truth, the question is even more bothersome than this. The lots are not only an instrument associated with our enemy; their symbolic meaning is profoundly disturbing. They seem to symbolize everything that traditional Judaism *doesn't* believe in.

Why? Well, lots are an instrument of chance. In casting lots to determine the day upon which the Jews would die, Haman was doing something rich with symbolic meaning: he was intentionally leaving the date of the Jews' demise up to chance. The Megilla even goes so far as to say that Haman cast lots not just to destroy us, but also to terrify us (Est. 9:24); the lots were an instrument of psychological warfare. It was as if Haman were taunting the Jews with the thought that whether they would live or die was not up to a providential God, but in the hands of blind fate. They were the prisoners of cold, hard chance. Such a vision is indeed terrifying.

If Jews and Judaism have stood for something over the years, it is for the opposite vision. In our worldview, the Almighty may prefer to stay hidden much of the time, but that doesn't mean He's not around; it just means you have to work to find Him. God is present in the workings of history. He's just behind the scenes. The historical events of Purim seem, themselves, to suggest this theological message. A number of apparent coincidences just "happen" to converge to bring about the salvation of the Jews. But are these events really just the product of blind chance?

Haman plotted to kill the Jews. But somehow events unfolded in such a way as to entrap him and foil his plans. Esther, a hidden Jew, was chosen queen of Persia by King Ahasuerus. Mordecai, her cousin and mentor, just happened to be in the right place at the right time, managing to overhear – and foil – an assassination plot against the king. The king just happened not to reward him immediately, allowing for that reward to be parceled out later, when it counted most. Later, on the very evening that Haman chose to come and ask permission to hang Mordecai, the king just happened to be unable to sleep. And just before Haman knocked on the door, the king – in order to conquer his sleeplessness – had asked for the Book of Records to be read to him. The book just happened to open to the right page, the page that recorded Mordecai's heroic efforts to safeguard the king from the would-be assassins, and the king was reminded of Mordecai's loyalty just in the nick of time. And the list goes on.

If you are a believing Jew, as the framers of Purim surely were, these serendipitous events were not really coincidences. They were not the product of blind chance. On the contrary, they were manifestations of God working in history, behind the scenes. If that's the case, the question we asked earlier is even more jarring: Why name the holiday after the very thing you *don't* believe in – coincidence and chance? The name of the holiday itself seems to be a bitter joke.

AREN'T THE ROYAL ROBES BESIDE THE POINT?

Besides the strange name for the holiday, there are many other mysteries in the Megilla. For the time being, I'd like to focus on a couple of meta-questions, questions that don't quite concern the Megilla's story itself, but how the Megilla *tells* us its story. One such question has to do with Mordecai, or more precisely, with the Megilla's apparent preoccupation with Mordecai. If you listen to the Megilla being read in the synagogue on Purim night, you will notice that there are several verses that by long-standing tradition are read aloud by the entire congregation in unison before the chazzan reads them from the actual Megilla scroll. It's hard to escape the impression that these verses signify something unusually important. So, what are these special verses? What do they talk about? Let's take a look. The first verse introduces us to Mordecai. It reads:

> There was a Jewish man who was in Shushan, the capital; his name was Mordecai, son of Yair, son of Kish; he was from the tribe of Benjamin. (Est. 2:5)

The second passage appears just after Haman is killed. It tells us that Mordecai went out in the streets dressed in royal blue robes with a big golden crown on his head, and that the city of Shushan erupted in joy (Est. 8:15). And the final verse read aloud by the entire congregation – the very last verse in the Book of Esther, as it happens – recaps Mordecai's rise to dizzying political heights. It reads:

> For Mordecai the Jew was second in charge to King Ahasuerus; he was great among the Jews, and pleasing to most of his brethren. (Est. 10:3)

Now here's a question for you. If it were up to you to pick a few verses to highlight in the Megilla, some verses that really get to the core of what Purim is all about, would it have been these particular verses? Forgive me if this sounds somewhat uncouth: these verses all focus, more or less, on Mordecai. They introduce us to him and celebrate his grandeur. But isn't that all a little beside the point?

It's not that I don't like Mordecai, or think he isn't worthy of praise. But still, the fact that Mordecai got to dress in royal robes and go out through the streets of Shushan in parade, or the fact that, after the Jews won the war, Mordecai remained second in charge to the king and was popular among his brethren – are these really the main things I'm celebrating on Purim? I would venture to say they are not. These things are nice, and they make us feel warm and fuzzy if we are fans of Mordecai, but that's not the point of the Megilla. The point of the Megilla, the reason we celebrate Purim, is that on that day, the Jews were miraculously saved from genocide. It's not because a particular Jew managed to attain, and retain, the trappings of success in a gentile society. Why then do we focus on these verses as if, somehow, the whole story revolved around them?

THE KING'S MAJESTY

We can ask a similar question about the Megilla's treatment of Ahasuerus, the Persian king. If you read the first twelve verses or so of the Megilla, you will find that they are all about the glory and grandeur of King Ahasuerus. We hear that he was emperor of the world, sovereign over 127 provinces stretching from India to Ethiopia. We hear about the king's lavish 180-day-long party. We hear about the riches everyone saw at those parties: the fine linens, the gold, the delicately fashioned utensils. If we were reading the royal archives of the Persian court, this would be understandable. But this is the Megilla we are reading – a Jewish book, not a Persian one. Why do I need to know all this? Why start a book in the Bible with such a banal, extended digression?

PLAYING "WHAT WOULD WE HAVE DONE?"

These are questions I've had about how the story is told: Why does the Megilla seem to last so needlessly long, and why does it seem to focus so inordinately on Mordecai's status and the king's grandeur? But let's leave these "meta-problems" aside for a moment. A slew of new difficulties awaits us within the text, concerning how and why major figures in the story acted the way they did.

In the next section of this book, we will begin to unearth these questions. But before we do, a quick word of caution: be aware that your familiarity with the Purim story will sometimes work against you. If you know the basic story line of the Megilla like the back of your hand, it can be hard for you to see the apparent strangeness in how the heroes and villains of the Purim story acted. When we know so well how Esther, Mordecai, the king, and Haman *actually* behaved, it is sometimes hard to imagine that they could have acted differently – but each of the Megilla's central figures surely could have.

In thinking about their actions, then, I would like to suggest that we do the following: Let's pause at strategic points in the Purim story, place ourselves in the shoes of any of the major figures in the narrative, and ask ourselves what we would do. When we arrive at an answer, we can then continue reading and compare what we would have done with what that person did in the real story. More often than not, I think we will be surprised by the gulf between what we expected to happen, and what actually did.

Before turning the page, you might give this a try. If you feel adventurous, pick a spot in the Megilla, set the scene carefully, then freeze the action, close your eyes, and step into the world of the royal court in ancient Persia. Mentally impersonate a character, then compare what you would have done with what he or she did. When you're finished, turn the page, and we'll compare notes.

Chapter Two

Why Did They Do That?

So now it's time to play Esther, Mordecai, Haman, and the king. What is surprising about how these people act?

WHY WAIT?

Let's start with Esther. She acts boldly, heroically – but also oddly. There is at least one moment, a crucial moment, when her course of action seems entirely inexplicable. Here is the background to that moment: Haman has issued his decree, setting a date (the fourteenth of Adar) when all Jews in the Persian Empire will be destroyed.

The Jews are mourning, and all seems lost. Mordecai, however, has an ace in the hole, and he decides that this is the time to play it. Esther has until now succeeded in maintaining a secret. She has never told the king that she is Jewish. Mordecai now implores her to reveal her secret. She must go to the king and beseech him to save her people.

Esther initially demurs. The king has sequestered himself for a while now in his private chamber – an inconvenient turn of events. According to the law of the realm, anyone who enters the king's chamber uninvited takes his life in his hands. Unless the king deigns to raise his scepter, allowing the visitor to enter, well, it's off with his head. Esther worries that this is not a propitious time to risk such a visit to the king; it's been a month now since he has called to see her, and she fears that she is no longer in his good graces. Perhaps Ahasuerus will use her unannounced appearance as an opportunity to do away with her. If so, her people's hopes will die along with her. Esther shares her concerns with Mordecai, but he won't take no for an answer. He insists that Esther go to the king, despite her misgivings.

So Esther gives in, and agrees to risk it all. She tells Mordecai that she and her ladies-in-waiting will undertake a prolonged, three-day fast, and then she will face the king, come what may. Three days come and go, and the moment of truth arrives.

Esther dresses in royal clothes and dares to enter the king's chamber. She catches the king's eye. He sees her, and – amazingly – he smiles and lifts his scepter, indicating permission to enter. As she approaches, he tells her that he will grant her request, no matter what it is. Up to half the kingdom and it's hers. "What do you need?" he asks.

OK; you play Esther. It's your move. What would you do? How would you reply to the king?

If I were Esther, this is the moment I would seize to make my request: *Well, you see, it's really very nice of you to offer half your kingdom, but actually, I just require a small favor. It seems that genocide has been decreed against my people. I don't know how it happened – some sort of palace mix-up, probably. But luckily, it's easy to reverse. If you wouldn't mind just signing right here, we can undo the decree right now – and I'd be ever so grateful.* That's what I would have said, at least. But it's not what Esther says. She doesn't use the moment to tell the king about the plight of the Jews, nor does she request that he annul the decree. Instead, she asks the king to meet her and Haman at a banquet she will hold later on. The question begs to be asked: Why does she do this? The king has lifted his scepter and offered to give her half his kingdom. She would have done *anything* just the day before for such a reception from him. She has no reason to expect she'll get the same welcome tomorrow. Why does she squander the magic of the moment by postponing the reckoning for some later time?

How does she know she will ever be in a better position than she is right now?

THE LADY DOTH PROTEST TOO MUCH

While we're talking about Esther, there's something else she does to confound our expectations. It has to do with her choice of time to cry.

There is a time when Esther actually throws herself at the feet of the king, cries, and literally begs him for mercy. Now, when does this happen? One would imagine it to take place at her most desperate hour, the time when things look darkest and most uncertain – perhaps when she first enters the king's chambers unannounced. Indeed, if there is any time her mission is most in danger, it is then. In a split second, the king will decide whether or not to raise his scepter, and the fate of both Esther and her people will be decided.

But that isn't when Esther cries. Neither does she cry later, when she rises dramatically at the banquet to indict Haman as the villain who would destroy her people. In neither of these moments, so fraught with danger, does Esther weep. When does Esther cry? Later, at a moment that appears far less dangerous, at a moment when, to all appearances, her battle has already been won.

The moment I am thinking of comes right after the death of Haman. It is a happy time, one would think. Not only has the king hanged his former vizier, he has also gifted Haman's house to

Mordecai as a reward for his loyalty. Things are certainly looking up for the Jews, wouldn't you say? Nevertheless, here is Esther throwing herself at the king's feet, weeping, pleading for mercy, begging the king to overturn Haman's genocidal decree. It all seems a little overwrought. The king has already gone so far as to kill Haman, formerly his most trusted advisor, and he has promoted Mordecai, leader of the Jews, to Haman's former office. He has even entrusted to Mordecai the royal signet ring, giving Mordecai, in effect, the final word on any legislation that would issue forth from the palace. The fortunes of the Jews have risen quite marvelously. But here is Esther, crying. What is she getting so teary-eyed about? Isn't the reversal of Haman's decree just a perfunctory administrative issue? In killing Haman, the king has clearly taken Esther's side. Why wouldn't he want to comply with Esther's very reasonable request to spare her people?

A COUNTERINTUITIVE ARGUMENT

It's time to talk about Mordecai. What does *he* do that confounds our expectations? Well, let's go back to a moment we've already examined from Esther's perspective, and review it this time from Mordecai's. We've talked about how Esther hesitated before going to the king. Let's discuss how, at that moment, Mordecai convinced her to take action. Here is what he told her:

> If you keep silent at this time, salvation will come to the Jews from somewhere else, and you and your father's house will be destroyed. And who knows if it was for this moment that you became queen? (Est. 4:14)

Mordecai makes a surprising argument here. Most of us, in his shoes, would have made an altogether different pitch. We would implore Esther to sacrifice herself, if necessary, for her people. After all, they *need* her; to whom else can they turn? But Mordecai says virtually the opposite: *You think we need you, Esther? We don't need you all that much. If you don't rise to the occasion, someone else will; salvation will come from elsewhere. God has many tools through which to effect His purposes.*

Now why does Mordecai say this? Here he is, trying to convince Esther that she *must* act, that her continued silence in the face of Haman's threat is not an option. How does he serve his purpose by telling her that the Jews will be fine without her? This seems, if anything, to give Esther an escape route, a chance to bow out gracefully from the scene. If Mordecai is really so confident that the Jews will be fine without Esther, what's to stop her from politely taking a pass and letting someone else ride heroically to the rescue? Isn't that exactly what he's trying to prevent?

THE PRICE OF COWARDICE

The next part of Mordecai's speech to Esther is just as strange. After telling her that if she doesn't act, someone else will, Mordecai adds – astoundingly – that if she fails to act, she will be destroyed:

> If you keep silent at this time... you and your father's house will be destroyed.

Destroyed? But why? To elaborate, had Mordecai been saying that Esther's assistance was crucial, that without it, the Jews would be lost, one could perhaps argue that if Esther were to withhold this crucial assistance, she would be culpable in a grand way. But that's not what he's telling her. He says the opposite: Esther is not crucial after all; one way or the other, the Jews will be saved. Why, then, should Esther's recalcitrance doom her to destruction?

Here's another way of looking at it: Let's say Esther stuck by her refusal to go to the king. It was just too dangerous, and she wouldn't be persuaded to do it. What's the worst you could possibly say of her?

If you wanted to be harsh, the worst you could accuse her of would be cowardice. By not going to the king, Esther would be exhibiting a failure of nerve; she would be acting without courage.

Now, let's talk about this. Since when, exactly, does one deserve to die for being a coward? As it happens, the Torah displays a remarkable tolerance for cowards: before going out to war, a priest would address the soldiers leaving for battle and urge anyone who felt fearful to leave the front and go home (Deut. 20:8). No one killed them because they were scared. On what grounds, then, could Mordecai threaten Esther with destruction for the mere crime of acting to safeguard her own life? And it's all the more inexplicable, given Mordecai's contention that Esther's actions are not crucial, that even without her, salvation would come to the Jews from another place.

PLUNDER NOT TAKEN

There's another difficulty we can raise concerning Mordecai's behavior, one that may seem trivial, but is worth studying: Mordecai propounds a royal decree that gives the Jews the right to defend themselves. Before we look at this issue, though, we need a little background information.

Throughout the history of warfare, it was the practice of victorious armies to plunder the possessions of their enemies. As the saying goes, "To the victor go the spoils." As a matter of fact, even modern battle plans have relied upon looting an enemy's resources while one advances, in order to supply one's army with needed food and fuel. During Hitler's offensive in the Ardennes, for example, the Germans' war plan depended upon the capture of enemy fuel depots to supply their own troops. In our story, however, the Jews buck this trend. More than once, the Megilla goes out of its way to tell us that the Jews took no plunder during their battles with those who would have killed them (see, e.g., Est. 9:10).

Now why did the Jews eschew what was "rightfully" theirs – the possessions belonging to their vanquished enemies? For a very good reason, as it happens, a reason with its genesis in the dawn of Jewish history. Haman, according to the Megilla, was a descendant of Agag, a king of Amalek who lived in the time of Israel's first king, Saul. The Five Books of Moses speak of the Amalekite nation and declare that the Jewish people will do battle against Amalek from one generation to another (Ex. 17:16). The war of Purim, then, seen in its broadest historical context, was just the latest iteration of this age-old war. And if you pay attention to the biblical rules governing war against Amalek, you know that there's one cardinal principle: there is to be no taking of spoils.

That principle comes through loud and clear in the book of Samuel. Centuries before Purim, King Saul was instructed by God to wipe out Amalek completely and to kill its king, Agag. Even their sheep and cattle were to be destroyed (I Sam. 15). Saul, however, failed to follow God's command. He allowed the people to take property from Amalek, and he did not kill Agag. Because of his failure, Amalek lived to fight another day. Later in history, when the Jews were exiled from their native land and found themselves under the sway of the Persian Empire, a notorious descendant of King Agag threatened them. Haman rose to power, and the Jews once again had Amalek to contend with. It makes sense, then, that in this battle against the forces of Haman, the Jews would be punctilious, and avoid taking any spoils of war. Keenly aware of Saul's folly, they were not going to make the same mistake twice. So the Megilla tells us over and over again that when the Jews vanquished their enemies in the time of Purim, no one took any spoils of war.

Yet something happens in Shushan that seems to "spoil" all of this. If you look carefully at the end of the Megilla, you will find that when Mordecai signs the royal decree authorizing the Jews to defend themselves, he specifically writes that the Jews are authorized, even encouraged, to plunder their enemies' possessions:

> And [Mordecai] wrote in the name of King Ahasuerus and sealed it with the king's ring…that the king had given to the Jews who are in every city [the right] to assemble and to protect themselves…and to take their enemies' spoils for plunder. (Est. 8:10–11)

Why would Mordecai do this? He, more than anyone, should know that this is a war against Amalek, that in this war the Jews would go to any lengths to avoid taking their enemies' possessions. And in fact, the Jews ignore his authorization: they don't take any spoils at all. Why, then, does Mordecai go out of his way to authorize the very thing he knows the Jews won't do?

We've taken a look at Mordecai and Esther and found many of their words and deeds puzzling. But it's not just the good guys whose actions seem inexplicable. The bad guys are just as hard to figure out.

A CURIOUS CALUMNY

Let's start with Haman, the archvillain of the story. He has decided to wage a pogrom against the Jews unprecedented in size and scope. He aims to wipe them out once and for all on a single day. In order to do this, though, he needs the consent of the king. So he goes before Ahasuerus to make his request.

Now, before we look closely at what he says, let's just take a moment to contemplate what we might have said had we been in Haman's position. What calumny could you dredge up against the Jews, what charge could you level against them that would be the most likely to incite the king's wrath and allow you to proceed with your murderous plot?

I can think of a lot of things Haman could've said: the Jews poison the wells, they bake the blood of Persian children into their matzos on Passover – you name it. Haman certainly doesn't feel constrained by the truth. As it happens, Haman says three things, but at least two of them seem entirely beside the point. Here are his complaints:

> The Jews are scattered throughout the Persian Empire.
> They observe their own laws, making them different from other nations.
> They don't keep the king's laws.

Now, why on earth does he bother with all this? If I were Haman, I would have dropped the first two points and mentioned only the third. It's the only one that seems likely to get the king's attention, the only one he's likely to care about.

Think about it: In his third complaint, Haman is basically arguing that the Jews are criminals, which is a logical approach; if the Jews are indeed criminals, if they don't keep the laws of the realm, then you could certainly argue that they deserve to be done away with. But who cares where, geographically, the Jews are? And who cares if the Jews observe a set of laws that distinguish them from other peoples in the kingdom? In all probability, the same could be said for every one of the king's 127 provinces. They *all* likely observed certain laws and customs that distinguished them from others. In all likelihood, the conquered people of India had different zoning laws than the people of Ethiopia – but is that grounds to do away with one or the other in a frenzied, state-sponsored bloodbath?[1]

---

1. One might make the argument that Haman was trying to depict the Jews as a kind of cancer on the body of Persia; in pointing out that they were scattered throughout the kingdom, then, he was raising the possibility that they were an insidious, constant presence that could somehow infect the entire realm with their lawlessness. The problem with this theory is that Haman's second charge – that the Jews "keep their own laws" – would seem to undercut his central argument. The Jews' observing their own laws, their insistence on being different, on maintaining their distinctiveness by allegiance to their own code, would tend to set them apart from everyone else and keep them separate. It would make the Jews less likely to insinuate themselves into

The more you think about it, the stranger Haman's choice seems: Why did he include those first two statements? They wouldn't seem to be the most potent, most damning things one could plausibly make up about these Jews. Presumably, though, Haman is not being foolish. He has a plan. He knows the king well, and the charges he is making are likely those that give him the greatest advantage. Our task is to figure out what he knew that we don't.

A QUEEN FOR ALL TO SEE

Finally, let's turn our gaze to King Ahasuerus. Many readers of the Megilla perceive Ahasuerus as a naïve, foolish ruler – and something of a boor, to boot. This perception arises, in part, from one of the very first scenes in the Megilla: the king seems to make an impetuous decision regarding his queen, Vashti. Ahasuerus, the Megilla tells us, has arranged for 180 of feasting and merrymaking in his capital city, Shushan, at the culmination of which he orders Vashti to be brought before the throngs and multitudes. According to the text, this is what he had in mind:

> He asked to have Vashti the queen brought before the king… to show off her beauty to the nations and princes – for indeed, she was very beautiful. (Est. 1:11)

Now what, exactly, was the king thinking? True, there's nothing surprising about a man taking pride in the beauty of his wife. And yes, a man at a party might delight in the stares his wife provokes from other men. But this is usually something that happens covertly, behind the scenes. Putting one's wife on display and inviting other

---

host cultures or to spread their culture to other peoples. If Haman's argument was that the Jews would "infect" everyone else, then why bring up the fact that they kept to their own laws?

men to marvel at her is just plain gauche, embarrassing not just for the poor woman at the center of attention, but for all the men in attendance, too. It's not a very royal, refined thing to do.

So why did Ahasuerus do it? Maybe he wasn't a very refined person. Maybe he was drunk. That's certainly possible, but I'd like to suggest an alternative. Perhaps there was a method to his madness. Perhaps if we take the time to understand things from Ahasuerus's point of view, we may well find that the king's course of action was not all that irrational.

If we can unravel this little mystery concerning the king and Vashti, we will gain valuable insight into many of the other conundrums we've pondered. We will begin to understand why Esther waited so long to make her plea, why she threw herself at the king's feet exactly when she did, why Mordecai's grandeur is such an essential part of the story – and why the Megilla lasts so long.

Let's take a stab at it.

Chapter Three

Mother Persia

Let's return to the question we raised earlier about Esther and her audience with the king. When Ahasuerus receives her graciously, extends his scepter, and says he will give her half the kingdom if she wants it, why does she wait? She has received the best welcome she could have imagined. She doesn't know if she will get the same welcome tomorrow. He's asked her what she wants. Why doesn't she just tell him? Why put off the inevitable?

Let's consider this question carefully, putting ourselves in Esther's shoes and evaluating her options. As Esther pondered how she would approach the king, what avenues would she have considered and rejected? Let's take a look at the possibilities that lay before her.

THE MORAL ARGUMENT

One approach Esther might have taken is to argue for the Jews on moral grounds, appealing to the king's sense of fairness and justice. I'll lay out the argument, and you tell me whether you think it would have worked: *Sire, a moral travesty is being carried out in the kingdom. An entire people has been unjustly accused, and they stand to be wiped out in a day of genocidal madness. We cannot let this stand. In the name of truth, justice, and the Persian way, please rescind this terrible decree.* What are the chances that this would have succeeded? It doesn't seem likely. Throughout the Megilla, the king doesn't seem particularly moved by concerns such as moral justice and fair play. Neither does he seem particularly concerned about the plight of his subjects; remember, when Haman asked the king to destroy the Jews, Haman didn't even name the nation he was seeking to obliterate:

> There is a people that is scattered among the other peoples… and it isn't worth it for the king to let them be. (Est. 3:8)

And the king allowed Haman to do whatever he liked to this anonymous nation:

> And the king took off his ring and gave it to Haman… and he said… "the nation is given to you to do what is fit in your eyes." (Est. 3:10–11)

Notice how casual it all is. *Here, take my ring. Do what you like, just don't bother me with these kinds of trivialities again; I'm late for lunch.* The king has decreed genocide against an entire people – and he's done it all with a disinterested wave of his hand.

If that's the way the king responded to Haman's request for license to kill, how might he respond to the queen's assertion that a moral crime was about to take place, that a nation in his realm had been unjustly accused? He might well have showed her the same kind of polite indifference he exhibited when he gave Haman his ring in the first place: *You know, Esther, minority affairs aren't really my thing. If you have some concerns about all this, I suggest you take them up with my secretary of state, a wonderful fellow by the name of Haman. I'm sure he'd be happy to help.* Clearly, the "moral travesty" approach is likely to fail. The king will not be compelled by the merit of the case. So if that's not going to work, what are Esther's other options? What other approach can she try?

THE OTHER OPTION

Seemingly, Esther has only one other option. If she can't ask the king to save the Jews on objective grounds, she must ask him to save them on *subjective* grounds. That is, she can ask the king to do her a personal favor. The king cares about her. He loves her. Let her ask him to spare her people for *her* sake.

It seems simple enough. Why doesn't she just do that? Why does she back off entirely and invite him to dinner instead? Evidently, Esther knows something that is giving her pause. What is it that she knows? She knows the terms on which she came to be queen.

To explain: If the king was apathetic about the Jews, there was one thing he was not apathetic about, one thing that had made him flaming mad. The king had asked Vashti, his previous queen, to appear and display her beauty at his party, and Vashti had demurred. When that happened, the king flew into a rage – and that was the end of Vashti. Esther knows this, and she knows that this incident has powerful implications, even now, for her own relationship with the king and for what she can plausibly ask of him.

To understand why this is so, we need to go back and confront some issues we raised earlier concerning the king and Vashti.

THE KING'S PROBLEM

Earlier, we wondered why the king would ask Vashti to display herself so publicly at the culmination of his party. It seems so gauche, so tastelessly overt. Let's return to that question now. I'd like to argue that there was a curious kind of rationality behind the king's demand. He might have been drunk, but he still had a plan.

The king had a plan because the king had a problem. To understand what it was, just read the very first verse of the Megilla:

> And it happened in the days of Ahasuerus – he was the Ahasuerus who ruled from India to Ethiopia, over one hundred and twenty-seven provinces. (Est. 1:1)

Put yourself in the king's shoes. It's the year 400 BCE or thereabouts. For centuries, the Babylonians had been the preeminent world power, but your people, the Persians, swept in like lightning and defeated them. The Persians then conquered even more territory and were soon the largest and most far-flung empire the world had ever seen. Then you, Ahasuerus, ascend to the throne. You find yourself sovereign over a breathtaking 127 provinces, spanning several thousand miles of landmass. What is your number one problem right now? Your problem is: How do you keep all of this together?

There is no Internet. There are no spy satellites. There are no telephones, fax machines, or even telegrams. There are no planes, cars, or trains. The fastest means of getting from place to place is on horseback. You are in charge of a global empire made up of 127 provinces. How, exactly, are you supposed to keep everyone in line? How are you to make sure that the various regional provinces remain loyal to the crown?

If the first verse of the Megilla sets forth Ahasuerus's problem, the very next verses set forth his answer: in a word, parties.

> [The king] made a feast for all his princes and his servants, the army of Persia and Media, the nobles and princes of the provinces, being before him; when he showed the riches of

> his glorious kingdom and the honor of his excellent majesty, many days, even 180 days. (Est. 1:3–4)

We asked earlier why the Megilla would elaborate so much about the pomp and circumstance of Persia. The answer is this: the Megilla does so not to celebrate Ahasuerus, but to tell a story. Pay attention to the little details in the verse, and you'll see the story emerge. Who gets invited to the feast? The nobles and the princes of all the provinces, the armies of Persia and Media. All the governors and middle management of little provinces scattered throughout the realm are coming to Shushan, the king's new capital city. And look what happens at the feast. The king shows off the splendor, glory, and might of the new empire. There are tapestries and linens, gold, wine flowing in the streets, excess everywhere. And don't forget: the army is there too. There are military parades with thousands of Persian soldiers falling in line behind officers, captains, and generals.

A strategy is unfolding here. If you were a minister in one of the outlying provinces – if you were the lieutenant governor of Turkmenistan, say – what reports would you bring home from the big convention you just attended in Shushan? It was quite a junket, all paid for with money from the federal coffers. You took your whole staff along; they all had a grand time, especially watching those elephants with the golden harnesses in the military parade. You were all dazzled by what you saw. What are you going to tell everyone about your trip?

You'll tell everyone about the grandeur that is the new Persia. When you are interviewed by reporters from the local newspapers, that's what you'll tell them, too. This new empire is really something, and you're glad to be a part of it.

The king knows what he's doing. He's consolidating his kingdom. The sparkle and sheen of the empire's economic and military might, leavened with a healthy dose of wine, will do more for his hold on power than any repressive laws, taxes, or forced loyalty program possibly could. Who wouldn't want to be part of the new Persia?

VASHTI'S CROWN

As Ahasuerus's 180-day feast draws to a close, he throws a second, culminating party that lasts seven days (Est. 1:5). And on the seventh and last day of this final party, he sends for Vashti, his queen, asking her to appear before everyone. Now, whatever else she was to wear or not wear (according to some midrashic traditions, the king asked her to appear unclothed),[1] there was one thing, according to the text, that she was certainly asked to wear: her crown. The verse makes a point of telling us about it:

> On the seventh day...the king said to...his seven closest servants...to bring Vashti the queen before the king, wearing the royal crown, and to display her beauty before the nations and the princes. (Est. 1:10–11)

Note whom the king sends to fetch Vashti – not your average palace hack or messenger boy. He dispatches his seven closest servants. A cabinet-level delegation makes its way over to bring Vashti to the party. And likewise, who is the intended audience for Vashti's beauty? It is not the common man, not your average Joe in the street. According to the text, the king put her on show for a very specific population:

> To display her beauty before the nations and the princes.

1. See, for example, Esther Rabba 4:14.

The "nations and princes" were to behold Vashti's beauty, a beauty accentuated by one particularly striking accessory: the royal crown. What is Ahasuerus doing?

AN AFFAIR OF STATE

Let's reflect for a moment about something. Who, or what, is a king? As head of state, a monarch wields enormous executive power. In the ancient world, the king's word was law; he held the power of life and death over his subjects. But a king is more than just a powerful executive. We can see this by looking at monarchies now in place throughout the modern world, where the crown is shorn of most of the regent's traditional power to govern. In today's Great Britain, for example, executive power resides in the office of the prime minister, legislative power in the House of Commons. Nevertheless, the monarchy still persists, and remains an important institution. Why? Because a king, quite apart from any executive power that he may or may not possess, is a living symbol of the nation he represents.

It has always been this way. Remember *Macbeth* and *Hamlet*? How does Shakespeare refer to kings in those plays? He calls them "Norway," for example, or "Denmark." The name of the nation becomes the name of the king. This is not a coincidence. The king is the body politic, a flesh-and-blood embodiment of the nation he represents.[2] The red carpets, the golden crowns, the grand parades – these are not for him as an individual. They

2. The Talmud (Kiddushin 32a–32b) states that a father or mother may waive the honor their children owe them, but a king may not waive the honor his subjects owe him. That is, a father can tell his daughter that she need not rise when he enters the room; a king cannot do the same for a subject. The Talmud explains the difference this way: a father and mother, as creators of their child, "own" the honor due to them, and can therefore forgo it if they wish. The king, on the other hand, does not "own" the honor due to him, so it is not his to forgo. The honor due the king is the honor of the nation. The people "own" this honor, not he.

are for the king as a symbol, a potent distillation into one man of the hopes, dreams, and aspirations of an entire people. A nation looks at its king and sees itself.

If the king is a symbolic embodiment of his country, what is the queen? The queen is the feminine embodiment of her country. In her persona, in her beauty, grace, and radiance, reside the beauty, grace, and radiance of an entire people. In Ahasuerus's case, his queen is Mother Persia. And at the culmination of his final party, he is showing off the final, most impressive symbol of his new empire: the beauty of Persia, embodied in the beauty of his queen, Vashti. Yes, the king is tipsy from the wine, and yes, he is objectifying his wife, treating her more as an object of beauty than as a person. But this objectification serves a political purpose, too. This is not an ordinary man showing off his girl to other men. This is an affair of state, presided over by the king's cabinet.

The queen, as object of beauty, is like a statue – a statue of the new Persia. We have a statue like that in modern times, too, right here in the United States, a female statue that embodies the aspirations, values, nobility, and beauty of our people; a statue that boldly and elegantly invites poor, huddled masses to find shelter beneath her outstretched arm. That statue strikes a resonant chord for most Americans. It means something to them. Americans do not think it strange to harbor a visceral, emotional attachment to Lady Liberty.

Ahasuerus wants Vashti to be that statue. The princes and provincial governors throughout the realm will look upon her with pride. They will revel in the beauty that is theirs, in the beauty that is Persia's. Through her elegance and grace, they will feel connected and committed to the empire she represents. Mother Persia will command the loyalty of her sons.

THE GIRL FROM NOWHERE

Vashti refuses to come, and for her sin, she forfeits her crown.[3] After this terrible affront, the king and his ministers decide it is now time for a new queen. The king begins a national search for the girl fit to be his new bride.

It is worth noting that, as his search progresses, the king betrays no special preference for a woman of noble blood. He does not seek to marry the daughter of a neighboring monarch. He does not even restrict his search to women of good Persian ancestry. This is truly an equal-opportunity beauty contest. Any girl can become the new queen. And perhaps that is only fitting. Once chosen, the queen will implicitly represent them all.

In the end, Esther is the king's pick. Why Esther? We don't know. The only overt information the text gives us is that "she found favor in the king's eyes" (Est. 2:17). But the text gives us one other tidbit about how she conducted herself with the king that may help us understand how she came to be so compellingly attractive to him.

Mordecai, Esther's cousin and mentor, had insisted throughout the whole beauty contest process that Esther not reveal her true identity. No matter what, she was not to tell the king that she was a Jew; she was not to divulge her family background:

> Esther did not tell of her people or of her birthplace, for Mordecai had commanded her not to tell this. (Est. 2:20)

---

3. The king's advisors counsel that Vashti must go, because if she stays, she sets a toxic example. Women will emulate her and defy their husbands. The social order will collapse. While to modern ears, the fears expressed by the king's advisors are somewhat silly and exaggerated, they seem to reflect an awareness that as the queen, Vashti really is Mother Persia. As first lady of the realm, her example matters. For better or for worse, what she says and does defines the values for which Persia stands.

Have you ever wondered how Esther got away with this? Eventually, at some point or another, Ahasuerus was going to ask her, "So, Esther, where are you from?" How was she supposed to respond? Let's say Esther smiles shyly and doesn't say anything. The king asks again, "No, seriously, where are you from? You have a really intriguing accent..." If she keeps smiling and changing the subject, the king is likely to get annoyed and just kill her. He's certainly shown a penchant for getting rid of uncooperative wives. How is Esther going to get away with this?

But amazingly, she does. The plan works. Esther actually manages to become queen without ever revealing her family, birthplace, or national identity. How did she do it?

Here's a theory: Maybe it was Esther's very refusal to talk about where she came from that helped endear her to the king. In the wake of the Vashti debacle, the king sought a girl who would succeed where his last wife had failed, a girl who would be everything Vashti was unable or unwilling to be. The king was looking for a woman who would effortlessly and unreservedly slip into the role of Mother Persia, who would happily and convincingly become the feminine symbol of his new empire. As such, Esther's recalcitrance might well have been alluring. Every time Esther changed the subject when the king asked her where she was from, she played into the king's dreamlike vision of the perfect queen: an utterly stateless girl, a woman who completely transcended whatever local or provincial identity fate had bequeathed her. Every time she smiled and said, "Why do you ask me so much about my past? Let's talk about the future," she would have seemed more and more like precisely the woman he was looking for. Esther could be from anywhere – or everywhere. Esther brimmed with possibility. She could be anything he wanted her to be.

ESTHER'S PREDICAMENT

The king falls in love with Esther, and she becomes his queen. For years, everything is perfect between them. And now, all of a sudden, Mordecai comes to Esther with a heart-stopping request. He tells her that, for the good of her nation, she must reveal her identity; she must tell the king she is a Jew and beg for her people's lives.

Esther goes to Ahasuerus. He sees her coming and smiles. He tells her she can ask for whatever she wants, even half the kingdom. But Esther hesitates and doesn't say the words. We asked why she avoided seizing that moment; where does her hesitation come from?

The answer is now evident. Mordecai's request has put the queen in a virtually impossible situation. Knowing what she knows about how the king views her, about how she assisted in cultivating that image, about what happened to Vashti – well, what exactly is she supposed to tell the king now?

Should she tell him that it was all a farce? That yes, she believes in his empire – long live the king, and all that, you know – but look, she has higher priorities. Her people (yes, she *does* have a people) are in danger; she cares about them tremendously, and would the king please help her out and save them?

I think we can all see how horrifically dangerous this would be. If, after years of smiling and suggesting that her own religious or national identity just doesn't matter, that she was the girl from nowhere, Esther turns around and reveals an intense affiliation with the Jews, she is likely to have her head handed to her. *What, it's not true? It never was? Your loyalty was with your own provincial sect all along?* The conversation with the king would only go downhill from there. The bottom line is this: if Esther pleads with the king to save her people, it is not likely to do anyone any good – not her, not her people. After all, *whose queen are you, Esther – ours, or theirs?*

Mordecai makes clear to Esther that silence is not an option.

She must act. But what can she possibly say?

Chapter Four

Obsession

DANGLING PRONOUNS

Esther doesn't remain silent, but she doesn't ask the king to save her people, either. Instead, she chooses a third option: she invites the king to a party. But she doesn't invite just him. She invites Haman, too.

> If I have found favor in your eyes, let the king and Haman come today to a banquet I have made for him. (Est. 5:4)

What is Esther doing here? As it turns out, a clue comes in the form of a grammatical incongruity in the verse. There is a subtle ambiguity in Esther's words, a dangling pronoun: "Let *the king and Haman* come today to a banquet I have made for *him*." Him, who?

Esther invites two people to this banquet, but then says she is making it for only one of them. Who, exactly, is the "him" that this banquet is for? There are only two possibilities, and if you're Ahasuerus, neither is especially appealing.

One possibility is that Esther is making the banquet for Ahasuerus. But if that's the case, why is she inviting Haman? What's he doing interrupting a private dinner for two? The other possibility, of course, is that the party is for Haman – but that possibility is even worse. Why is she making a party for him?

Things only get worse once the banquet actually takes place. At the feast, the king again asks Esther to tell him what's on her mind. Up to half the kingdom, and he's happy to give it to her. *Just tell me, Esther, and it's yours.* Esther's response? She seems almost surprised that the king has asked her what's on her mind:

> My request and my petition? If I have found favor in the eyes of the king and if it please the king to grant my petition, and to perform my request, let the king and Haman come to [another] banquet that I shall make for them, and I will do tomorrow as the king has said. (Est. 5:7–8)

Now go back and check the pronouns. Notice anything? "Let the king and Haman come to [another] banquet that I shall make for *them*." Now, all of a sudden, Esther uses the plural. The banquet is for both of them, both the king and Haman. Things are in flux. Whoever the banquet was for the first time, the king *or* Haman, it's changed now. Now it's for the king *and* Haman. What, exactly, does Esther think she is doing here?

SHARED DESTRUCTION

Stop and ask yourself: How would you characterize Esther's choices here? Would you call them safe or hazardous?

Esther is planting the seed of an exceptionally dangerous idea in the mind of the king. As Rashi, grandfather of the medieval commentators, suggests, Esther is insinuating, without quite saying it, that perhaps something is going on between her and

Haman. If we look at what she is doing without the benefit of hindsight – without knowing that in the end, things work out for her – it would seem that Esther is embarking on something close to a suicide mission. In Persia during the fourth century BCE, what is the average life span of a queen whom the king suspects of adultery?

Why is she being so imprudent? Evidently, Esther has concluded that she has little choice. If the king perceives Esther to be involved with Haman, then maybe they will both hang on the royal gallows before the banquet on the morrow – and if that's what happens, so be it. She will at least have brought the Jews' tormentor down with her, and perhaps her people will somehow emerge whole from Esther and Haman's shared demise.

THE ONLY THING WORSE THAN KNOWING IS NOT KNOWING

Having embarked on this perilous path, Esther plays the part to the hilt. Not only does she suggest the possibility of a dalliance with Haman, she cloaks that possibility in ambiguity. Who is the first banquet for? Could be for the king, could be for Haman. And then a second invitation for *them*, for both the king and Haman. If the king is trying to figure out what's going on, he's pursuing a moving target.

Often, when we find ourselves faced with difficult or dangerous circumstances, the most unbearable part is not the danger itself, but the uncertainty associated with it. When the doctor says that something is seriously wrong, but he doesn't know what it is, he needs to order more tests – that's when the patient's blood pressure skyrockets. When, in a horror novel, the victim walks slowly through the corridors of an empty house and nothing happens yet that's the most frightening part of the book. From the king's perspective, the worst part is *not knowing*. Who is the banquet for? Either possibility is bad, but what's even worse is not knowing which it is. And as if that weren't enough, whatever the reality was yesterday, it's changed today. Then, of course, the final uncertainty: *Maybe I misheard her. Maybe she just stumbled over her words. Why am I letting my imagination get the best of me? Why am I making such a big deal over nothing?* It's no wonder the king can't sleep that night.[1]

> That night the king couldn't fall asleep, and he asked that the book of chronicles be brought before him to be read to him. (Est. 6:1)

"YOU'LL NEVER GUESS WHO I SAW ON MY WAY OUT OF THE PALACE"

If the king leaves the banquet in a state of agitation, Esther's other invitee, Haman, leaves without a care in the world. Until, at least, he reaches the palace gates:

> Haman left the banquet joyous and carefree. But when Haman saw Mordecai, who was seated in the court of the king, [and perceived that] he did not rise, or even move whatsoever [in deference to Haman] – [when he saw this], Haman was filled with rage at Mordecai. (Est. 5:9)

Responding to Mordecai's affront, Haman goes home, assembles his wife and close friends, and pours out his heart to them. As evil as Haman is, if you listen carefully to what he says here, it's hard not to feel sorry for him. Haman tells them all how rich he is, how many children he has, and how the king has elevated him to the pinnacle of power. With an irony that only we, the readers, can appreciate, Haman gives as ultimate proof of his success the fact that he, and

1. See Rashi to 6:1. Rashi quotes a source attributing the king's insomnia to suspicions of a dalliance between the queen and Haman.

only he, is invited back for a second private banquet with the queen and king. Yet all this, he concludes, somehow seems hollow:

> But all of this [glory] is worth nothing to me whenever I see Mordecai the Jew sitting in the gates of the palace. (Est. 5:13)

Look how pitiful this man is. Haman has everything. He is on top of the world. But in his own mind, he can take no pleasure in any of it as long as there is *one person in the world* who won't bow to him. Keep in mind, by the way, who Haman has been talking to. He tells his wife and closest friends how many children he has and how rich he is. Wouldn't they, of all people, know this already? What kind of person has to tell his wife how rich he is? To those listening to him, Haman must have sounded vaguely silly, to say the least. But Haman himself, single-mindedly consumed with his Mordecai problem, doesn't know, or doesn't care.

POISONED MEDICINE

After Haman reveals his frustrations with Mordecai to those gathered around him, his wife, Zeresh, proposes a solution that she thinks will give her husband some peace of mind:

> Zeresh his wife said to him: "Let a gallows be prepared, fifty cubits high, and in the morning, you'll go to the king – and you'll hang Mordecai on the gallows. [That way] you'll come with the king to the banquet feeling happy and in a good mood. (Est. 5:14)

Zeresh has found some Tylenol for Haman. Why, she asks him, should you have to go to the banquet in a sour mood? Why suffer, when an effective remedy is so close at hand? Come now, a little bloodletting is good for the spirit. Just build the gallows and call me in the morning.

Haman goes eagerly to prepare the gallows and approach the king. But by giving in to Zeresh's advice, he has, ironically, defeated the entire purpose of his pogrom. Consider this: Why does it take Haman until chapter 5 of the Megilla to figure out that he could just ask the king to hang Mordecai? He has always hated Mordecai; why wasn't killing him the very first item on Haman's agenda? The Megilla itself provides the answer to this question: Haman thought it too petty to kill Mordecai alone (Est. 3:6), so he decided on a pogrom against his entire people, the Jews.

When you're second in charge to the king, getting rid of the fellow in the bleachers who refuses to bow when your motorcade passes seems somehow beneath you. It's doesn't befit a man of Haman's stature to care so deeply about such things. So what does Haman do instead? He concocts a plan to wipe out Mordecai's entire people – and in so doing, he will get Mordecai as well. The pogrom will provide the cover he is looking for; he won't seem petty anymore. He'll say the Jews are lawbreakers, that for the good of society, they must be disposed of. It will be a matter of national security. In the end, an entire people will die so that Haman can get to Mordecai without it seeming "personal." Now, though, Haman's artfully constructed façade reveals a crack. In making the gallows in his backyard for his nemesis, Haman betrays the truth – it really *is* all about Mordecai; it's been personal all along. The plan to commit genocide is now hollow. Its central rationale is gone. In his zeal to do away with the man who will not bow to him, Haman has, in the end, sacrificed the appearance of respectability he worked so hard to cultivate. As we shall soon see, this sacrifice will later come back to haunt him.

A HASTY AUDIENCE WITH THE KING

Let's return now to the unfolding story. When we last left Haman, Zeresh was suggesting that he ask the king to terminate Mordecai. What is Haman's response to her advice? At first, it seems like he listens to her. He runs to make the gallows and heads to the king to ask permission to hang Mordecai. But if you look carefully, you will find that Haman doesn't take her advice – at least, not exactly.

Zeresh had counseled her husband to go to the king in the morning and ask him to hang Mordecai (Est. 5:14). Look, though, when Haman actually goes to the king:

> That night, the king couldn't sleep… and the king said [to his chamberlains]: "Who is in the courtyard?"… the king's servants said to him: "It is Haman standing in the courtyard!" (Est. 6:1–5)

Haman never even waited for morning. It's the middle of the night. The king has already retired to bed. And there is Haman, out in the darkness, getting ready to throw pebbles at the king's window. What, exactly, does he think he's doing? For all Haman knows, Ahasuerus is long since asleep. How thrilled will the king be to be awakened so Haman can ask him if, pretty please, it's okay to hang Mordecai now? Haman simply cannot wait. This has to be done right now.

The Haman we used to know would never have acted this way. Haman had always been very conscious of appearances. He was quite delicate with the king, for example, in asking permission to destroy the Jews. He never named the nation that was the target of his enmity, and he used euphemisms to describe the dirty task of killing; Haman speaks of those who would carry out the massacre as "doers of the work" (Est. 3:9). Suddenly, though, all that has changed. Haman unabashedly delivers a soliloquy to family and friends about his riches and his many children, and now, just as unabashedly, he turns up for an unannounced midnight tête-à-tête with the king. So obsessed is Haman with Mordecai that he seems unable to perceive what he actually looks like to everyone around him.

THE MAN THE KING WANTS TO HONOR

As fate would have it, Haman and Ahasuerus, two men who cannot sleep, meet that night. Haman was unable to sleep because he was preoccupied with Mordecai. But sleep has eluded the king, for he too has been preoccupied – with Haman. *Why is the queen inviting him to all these banquets with me?* Each man is locked in his own thought-world, each preoccupied with someone else.

Here's how their encounter unfolds: As the king lies awake, he asks for the book of royal records to be opened and read to him. It's at least as good as counting sheep. But lo and behold, the book reveals a surprise: it opens precisely to the record of a long-forgotten deed carried out by Mordecai.

Long ago, Mordecai had overheard two palace servants plotting to assassinate Ahasuerus. Mordecai foiled the plot, and his act of loyalty was duly recorded in the king's records. Now, as the king lies awake, he listens as Mordecai's deeds are retold to him, and he stops to ask whether Mordecai was ever rewarded for saving his life. The servant reading the book checks and replies in the negative, and just then, the king perceives that someone is out there, in the dead of night, in the outer courtyard of the palace. He asks who it is, and is informed that it is Haman. Ahasuerus asks for Haman to be brought in, and before Haman can say a word about Mordecai, the king preempts him with a request of his own.

"What," the king wants to know, "should be done with a man the king wants to honor?" If the query catches Haman off guard, he doesn't show it; he quickly assimilates the question and draws the only conclusion that makes any sense to him, at least from his own limited frame of reference:

> Haman said in his heart: "To whom would the king want to bestow greatness and honor more than me?" So Haman said to the king: "The man the king wants to honor? Let them bring royal clothes that the king has worn and a horse that

> the king has ridden upon and upon whose head the royal crown has been placed. And let the clothes and the horse be presented [to him] by one of the king's high ministers, and let them dress the man the king wants to honor in the clothes, and let them parade him through the streets on the horse, and let them call before him: 'Thus shall be done to the man whom the king wishes to honor!'" (Est. 6:6–9)

If you were in the king's shoes, what would you think of Haman's response? Look over Haman's words carefully and count how many times the word "king" or "royal" appears in his statements. It's all "king, king, king."

So if you were Ahasuerus, and already couldn't sleep that night because you were worried that Haman was after your wife, and then Haman walked into your room in the middle of the night and gave you this advice, what would you be thinking? You could be excused for thinking: *Not only does he want my wife... he wants my job, too. He wants the crown.*[2]

---

2. As a matter of fact, it's even worse than this. The king's lurking suspicion about adultery may have been reinforced by Haman's words. Look what Haman says about the clothes and the horse provided for the person the king wants to honor: not just royal clothes and a royal horse, but a horse the king has ridden upon and clothes the king has worn – personal implements of the king, things the king has actually used. Haman is suggesting that the greatest honor one could bestow upon a commoner would be for him to have use of items the king himself has made use of. (See in this regard Rambam, *Hilkhot Melakhim* 2:1, who states that the honor of a king demands that his personal articles be burned after his death, so that others may not make use of them.)

   So Haman is implying he would like to use the king's private stuff. But what is the greatest "personal implement" of all? Ahasuerus is left to wonder: Is it just about the clothes the king has worn and the horse the king has ridden upon, or does this fascination with "that which the king has used" extend beyond this, too? Does it extend to his wife, to the queen? If the king wondered whether Haman was after Esther, Haman's words could only have reinforced this fear (cf. Rambam, above, 2:2).

A PRISONER OF THE HEART

Barbara Tuchman, in her book *The March of Folly,* details how leaders of nations sometimes inexplicably but doggedly pursue courses of action that run counter to their own interests. They become their own worst enemies. What is the source of Haman's particular brand of folly? The Megilla seems to tell us. "Haman said in his heart: 'To whom would the king want to bestow greatness and honor more than me?'" (Est. 6:6). In a curious way, Haman has fallen victim to a lack of imagination. Haman is literally incapable of imagining that the king might want to honor anyone but him. As we saw before in his words to Zeresh about his wealth and children, Haman is in his own world, and is virtually imprisoned there; he has lost the ability to perceive what he sounds like to everyone around him.

The Midrash (Genesis Rabba 34:10) expresses this pithily and poignantly. It suggests that the difference between a wicked person and a virtuous one is that a wicked person is "in the domain of his heart," and a virtuous one keeps his "heart in his own domain." That is, a wicked person is locked inside his heart, a veritable prisoner of his own emotions, whereas a righteous person is "outside" his desires in the sense that he exerts control over them. This is expressed, according to the Midrash, by the language the Bible uses to describe wicked people who speak to themselves. The expression invariably used is *vayomer belibo,* "he said in his heart." The Midrash sees in this formulation the idea that the speaker is speaking from *within* his own heart, as it were, as if he were the prisoner of his heart, of his desires. As evidence of this phenomenon, the Midrash points to Haman, who spoke "in his heart" in the passage we have been considering.

> Haman said in his heart: "To whom would the king want to bestow greatness and honor more than me?" (Est. 6:6)

Haman is indeed the prisoner of his desires; he cannot see beyond them or hear how strange his words sound to others. The king listens, aghast, to Haman's words. From his perspective, Haman has made his intentions perfectly clear. He wants the king's things; he wants the king's crown. It is no surprise, then, that the king responds as he does:

> Quickly – take the horse and the clothes as you've said, and do this all for Mordecai the Jew who sits in the court of the king. Don't withhold any of the things you've spoken about! (Est. 6:10)

And that's what happens. Haman leads Mordecai through the streets on the horse, personally conducting a parade of honor for his mortal enemy.

At first glance, it may seem strange for the king to ask Haman to personally orchestrate the parade, to personally lead Mordecai through the streets on the horse. It's one thing to accept Haman's advice about how honor should be bestowed. It's another to ask Haman to be the one to lead the horse through the streets. What's the king doing asking his secretary of state to go be a stable boy? Weren't there any other servants around? But maybe that's actually the point. The king wants Haman in particular to be the one to lead around this "man the king wants to honor." From Ahasuerus's perspective, it's not such a terrible thing for Haman's balloon to be deflated a bit.[3] A little humility does wonders for the soul.

By the time Esther's second banquet rolls around, Haman is no longer in quite the position of power he had occupied just a day earlier. The man who was formerly Ahasuerus's closest advisor has, through a combination of his own words and Esther's actions,

---

3. Yoram Hazony makes this point convincingly in his excellent book *The Dawn: Political Teachings of the Book of Esther* (Shalem Press, 2000).

come under the suspicion of the king. Haman, all but invincible just a day before, is now perhaps vulnerable. As the table is set and the wine poured for her second banquet, it is up to Esther to seize the moment somehow, without getting herself killed in the process.

Chapter Five

Martial Arts

Despite Haman's newfound vulnerability, it will not be easy for Esther to make her case to the king. She is beset by two major challenges and must find a way to deal with each. First, there is her "Mother Persia" liability: should she reveal her nationality and throw her lot in with her people, the "girl from nowhere" risks being seen as a charlatan by the king, or even worse, a traitor. Above and beyond that, she has planted the suspicion of adultery in the mind of the king. If the first liability would make her a traitor on the national stage, the second would make her a traitor on a private, personal stage. To some extent, Esther is battling these two liabilities as much, or more, than she is battling Haman himself.

HOW THE WEAK CAN WIN

Yet as overwhelming as these liabilities might seem, Esther is not doomed to succumb to them. To draw an analogy from hand-to-hand combat, a weak combatant is not always destined to lose the fight. With the right technique, he or she can win.

What's the right technique? The martial arts were founded to address this question. If you are overwhelmingly strong, you don't need the martial arts. You just walk right out and squash your opponent. It is the weaker combatant who truly needs karate or jujitsu. Using the finely honed techniques espoused by these systems, weaker fighters can indeed defeat opponents who possess more brute force than they do.

I'm not an expert in the martial arts myself, but from the little I know of them, virtually all of these systems advocate some variation of the following basic strategy: *Do not pit your strength against the strength of your opponent. Rather, find a way to use your opponent's own strength to bring about his downfall.*

To see this technique in action, watch the way a student of karate defends himself against an attacker. If a punch is thrown his way, he does not thrust his palm forward to meet his opponent's fist. If he did that, he would directly confront his enemy's power, and if he were the weaker one, he would lose. Instead, he will move his arm at an angle, slightly diverting, rather than stopping, the force of the punch. When he does this, his opponent's fist misses its mark, and continues moving past him in almost the same trajectory it started on. As his opponent follows through on the punch, striking nothing but air, he staggers forward and is thrown off-balance. The next move is then obvious. Just push the opponent, gently diverting his force, and get out of the way. With the attacker already off-balance, that little nudge can be enough to knock him off his feet.

If Esther is to avoid getting squashed by the liabilities she faces, she needs to employ something like the above strategy. Somehow, she must "get out of the way" and gently divert the momentum of the substantial power arrayed against her. That is, she must take the king's fear that she is involved in an illicit relationship, and his anticipated anger at the discovery that she is not the "Mother Persia" he hoped her to be, and divert these forces so that they work in her favor, not against her. But that's a tall order. How is she supposed to do that?

THE WHITE KNIGHT AND THE QUEEN

Let's watch and see. As the second banquet unfolds, Esther, Haman, and the king are seated. The food is served; the wine is poured. Ahasuerus asks Esther, as he did a day before, to make her request – up to half the kingdom, and he is prepared to grant it. This time, Esther tells him what's really on her mind. Here is what she says:

> If I have found favor in the king's eyes, and if it pleases the king, give me my life as my request, and [the life of] my people as my petition. For I and my people have been sold – to be destroyed, killed, and annihilated. (Est. 7:3–4)

The king, stammering, demands to know who would dare do such a thing, to which Esther replies:

> A man who is a treacherous enemy: Haman, this evil one. (Est. 7:6)

So there it is: Esther finally reveals that her people, the Jews, are endangered, and she brings to light the identity of the aggressor, Haman. It all seems very straightforward. But go back and examine more carefully what she said. How is Esther dealing with her two liabilities?

A first clue comes from the fact that Esther has not simply asked the king to spare her nation. She has asked him to spare her *own* life too. Moreover, she mentions her own life first:

> Give me my life as my request, and [the life of] my people. (Est. 7:3)

The news that someone is out to get his queen, that Esther's own life is threatened, has immediate shock value for the king. It makes everything she says after this pale into comparative insignificance. Only one question matters to him: "Who is trying to do this to you?" Of course, Esther is only too happy to share the answer:

> Haman, this evil one. (Est. 7:6)

In her pronouncement, Esther has couched the revelation that she is a Jew – that she belongs to a particular people with whom she still identifies – inside the most explosive news imaginable: someone is out to kill her. The announcement of her national affiliation, which in any other circumstance would have been headline news, has been virtually drowned out by an even bigger headline: *someone is out to kill the queen.* For Ahasuerus, it's even more personal than that: *someone is out to get my wife.*

As a first step in softening the threat to her Mother Persia image, Esther has distracted Ahasuerus from thinking about her possibly divided national loyalties by giving him something even more compelling to think about. The woman he loves is asking him to rescue her. He has the chance to play the knight in shining armor. What kind of man wouldn't rise to the occasion?

THE DAMSEL WHO CAUSED HER OWN DISTRESS

Lost in the drama of the moment, of course, is an inconvenient little fact: if you really stop and think about it, Esther's claim that her life is threatened isn't 100 percent true. Go ahead, work it out: Is it really accurate to say that Haman is trying to kill her? That claim might *sound* good, but it's not going to win any awards for journalistic integrity. Haman didn't even know she was a Jew. No one – the king included – knew she was a Jew until just now, when Esther volunteered this information. So yes, now that she has, of her own accord, divulged her religion and national identity, she is, technically speaking, threatened by Haman's blanket decree of genocide. But that threat to her own life is of her own making. She could have just kept quiet. Moreover, even now that she has divulged her identity, is she really threatened? She's the queen, for goodness' sake. The king could easily issue her a pass, excluding her from the carnage that will befall everyone else. Esther's claim that she is imperiled is, once you stop to think about it, highly dubious.

For her part, though, Esther hopes the king won't stop to think about it. She wants him to act quickly and passionately, without contemplating the complexities of the situation. She wants him to countermand the decree that is causing all the trouble, saving her and tangentially (as far as the king is concerned) saving the rest of the Jews as well. Esther's words direct Ahasuerus to the hasty conclusion she wants him to draw: *If the queen is threatened by a man who would destroy her because of her national affiliation, why not just annul the decree that threatens her, kill the man who thought it all up, and save her life*? There you go, the logic works perfectly! As long as you don't think about it too much.

HAMAN IS SO YESTERDAY

By cloaking her status as a Jew inside the more arresting news that someone is trying to kill her, Esther takes a first step toward insulating herself from whatever fallout her revelation of religious and national identity might create. But Esther goes beyond this, too. She doesn't just distract the king from her disclosure of a particular provincial affiliation with other, more compelling news; in true martial-arts fashion, she turns that disclosure of provincial affiliation against her opponent.

How does she do this? Well, let's revisit what we have called Esther's "Mother Persia" problem. Esther knows that the king is looking to her, as he did to Vashti before her, to be the feminine symbol of his new empire. She knows she has presented herself as the girl from nowhere, willing and able to assume this symbolic role. She knows, therefore, that if she betrays a narrow, provincial allegiance, she risks destroying herself, along with the group that commands her loyalties. Those are the constraints under which she must work.

Look carefully at Esther's words. Even as she implicitly reveals herself as a Jew, has she crossed any of these red lines? Has she shown herself disloyal to the grand vision expected of "Mother Persia"? The answer, astoundingly enough, is no. If anything, Esther portrays *Haman* as the one disloyal to that vision.

Ingeniously, by casting Haman's decree as an edict that above all threatens her own life, Esther has made Haman into the villain – the racist, as it were – who won't accept her as queen of all. Haman, not Esther, is the one who is stuck in a tribal mindset, who won't accept the king's enlightened new way of looking at the girl he made his queen. Esther is still exactly who the king wants her to be. Her position remains what it always was: she and the king share the dream of a pan-Persian empire transcending race and narrow, petty national allegiances. Of course, everyone comes from *somewhere*, but why should anyone concern himself with any of that? It's a new world, and racial and provincial allegiances are *so* yesterday.

There's only one person in the room, Esther is saying, who doesn't agree with all this, who doesn't see the world in the enlightened way we do, and that's Haman. Haman is trying to kill me, along with all other Jews, because of nothing more than our ethnic identity. He is so caught up in labeling people by group, race, or ethnicity that he can't look past my provincial roots to see me for the queen I am, for the queen you want me to be. Please understand, sire: there's only one person in this room who refuses to see me as Mother Persia. *That person is Haman!* Esther has deftly moved out of the way and allowed the freight train of the Mother Persia issue to barrel past. Haman is now the one stuck on the tracks, staring into the oncoming headlights.

"Mother Persia" is no longer a liability for Esther. It is an asset.

MAKING A FRIEND OF FAITHLESSNESS

How does Esther respond to her other liability, the king's suspicion that she may have been faithless to him, that she may be involved in a dalliance with Haman?

At first glance, she seems to confront and refute this suspicion head-on. She identifies Haman as her enemy, as an evil man who will destroy her and her people. It seems pretty clear that she has no warm feelings for him; Esther and Haman are decidedly uninvolved with one another. So she just flat-out refutes the king's suspicions about her and Haman, right? A closer inspection, though, will reveal otherwise. In true martial-arts style, Esther doesn't so much refute the king's fear as divert it; she makes it work for her, not against her. How so? Well, let's revisit the scene at the second banquet, looking at it from the king's perspective. Going into that banquet, if Ahasuerus was in fact suspicious that Haman was romantically pursuing his queen, how would he have formulated that suspicion to himself?

He would have looked at Haman as someone who was, potentially, trying to take his wife away from him.

Now, if *that's* what the king was saying to himself – *Haman is trying to take her away from me* – Esther confirms the king's worst fears. She is, in effect, saying, "Yes, he *is* trying to take me away from you, just like you thought. You were worried that Haman wanted to deprive you of your queen? Well, that's exactly what he's trying to do. No, he's not going to do it through romance; instead, he's going to do it by killing me – but let's not get distracted by the fine points. One way or another, the core of what you suspected is true. *He's going to try to take me away from you.*" Esther has taken the king's suspicion of adultery and gently diverted it. All the energy and sublimated rage the king had felt over the possibility that Haman was seducing her is now free to express itself as fury over the discovery that Haman was trying to kill her. Bloodshed, romance – why quibble over details? Bottom line: *Haman's trying to take her away from me*. Once again, an overpowering force was headed in Esther's direction, and she managed to give it a little nudge and step out of the way, leaving Haman directly in its path.

THE WRONG TIME FOR A WALK IN THE GARDEN

When Esther identifies Haman as the evil architect of the decree that would kill her, the king bolts to his feet, enraged. Haman cringes. And then? Well, then the king abruptly disappears. He walks out of the banquet and goes for a stroll in the garden to think things over. If you were Esther, how happy would *you* be about this latest development?

Until now, the king has consistently dispatched every decision that has come his way with a minimum of thought and deliberation. Here, too, Esther had been counting on the king to respond impetuously. She wants him to kill Haman immediately and annul his decree in one fell swoop, all in the service of saving his imperiled queen. But now, just this once, the king actually decides to think things over before acting. It's the worst possible luck. If the king starts thinking, he may just realize any number of inconvenient truths – including the fact that he doesn't really need to annul Haman's decree to save his wife. Alas, deliberate thought on the part of the king is the one thing that could collapse the fragile narrative Esther has so painstakingly constructed. The king's abrupt decision to exit the banquet leaves Esther vulnerable in another way. It leaves her alone in the room with a wounded and cornered enemy. Haman will now have a few precious minutes alone with Esther – and if he uses them well, victory, even at this late hour, could yet be his. At this delicate moment, let's step aside to contemplate the nightmare scenario that could unfold at the banquet table while an absent king paces in the garden, mulling over the implications of Esther's desperate plea.

Chapter Six

The Backyard Gallows

What did Haman say to Esther during those minutes the king was away in the garden? The Megilla doesn't tell us, so we will never know. But when we step back to contemplate what Haman could have said, we may find ourselves surprised by the potential of the arguments at his disposal. He could well have made those few minutes exceedingly uncomfortable for Esther.

HAMAN'S CURIOUS RATIONALE FOR GENOCIDE

To fully appreciate the strength of Haman's position, even at this point in the story, we must go back and revisit a question we raised earlier. We asked why, when Haman initially went to Ahasuerus for license to exterminate the Jews, he chose to lodge three apparently disconnected complaints against them: the Jews are dispersed, their laws are different from others, and they don't keep the king's laws. We argued that the first two complaints seemed irrelevant; what does the king care whether the Jews are localized in one spot or spread out? And what does he care whether or not they cling to a set of quaint, provincial customs?

Haman could have saved his breath, we argued, and offered only the last of his complaints, since presumably it was the only one Ahasuerus really cared about. If the Jews really lived in wholesale disregard of the king's laws – well, that would anger any self-respecting sovereign. So why did Haman bother mentioning his other two gripes?

In truth, the question goes even farther. Haman's third charge, if true, would seem to *demand* a response on the part of the empire. If the Jews were really flouting the king's laws, the crown could not reasonably tolerate the situation; the Jews would have to be destroyed – or at least subdued. But for some reason, Haman takes a much milder position on the imperative of doing away with the Jews. He tells Ahasuerus that *it's not worth it* for the king to leave them be. Why would Haman pull a rhetorical punch like this? If he wants to do away with the Jews, and is making the claim that they are lawbreakers, shouldn't he follow through by arguing that the king cannot *afford* to leave the Jews around? Why make the less forceful claim that *it's not worth the king's while* to leave them around?

The answer to all of this is that we've misunderstood Haman; he was not making three separate complaints against the Jews. He was making a single, unified complaint – a complaint that had three parts and was built on three interlocking premises. When he spoke to the king, Haman laid out those three premises and left the larger argument to the king's imagination. The larger argument didn't have to be stated explicitly; it emerged organically from what he said. Indeed, if you add up the three premises, the conclusion – that it just *wasn't worth it* for the king to let the Jews be – becomes self-evident, virtually inescapable. What, exactly, was that larger argument? Let's piece the premises together and watch it emerge.

OUT OF THREE, ONE

Haman begins his address this way:

> There is a certain nation that is scattered and dispersed throughout the other nations. (Est. 3:8)

Notice that the word "nation" appears at both the beginning and the end of that sentence: a certain *nation* is scattered among the other *nations*. What's the implication? Nations, by definition, have boundaries; this one is here, and that one is there. They are separate from one another. But not *this* nation; this one is scattered all over the place. Haman continues:

> And their laws are distinct from other nations.

When you stop and think about it, what makes any nation a nation? What are the bare-bones requirements for nationhood? It seems fair to say that there are at least two bedrock requirements. A nation needs some land, and it needs a system of governance. Everything else – distinct language, a sophisticated culture, unique accents, tourist attractions – all this is nice, but it's gravy. The essentials are land and laws.

Well, what about the Jews? It turns out that the Jews are different from all the other 127 provinces of the king's empire. They may have laws, but they don't have any land. At least, they don't anymore.

Haman is referring obliquely to a very recent development in the history of these Jews. For the past several centuries, the Jews had indeed possessed land of their own. They lived as a sovereign people in the land of Israel. Then, just a few generations before Haman emerged on the scene, all of that changed. Sennacherib, king of Assyria, conquered the Northern Kingdom of Israel and sent those tribes into exile. The Southern Kingdom, the Kingdom of Judah, managed to persist a while longer. But then they, too, fell to outside conquest: Nebuchadnezzar of Babylon invaded, conquered Jerusalem, burned the Temple to the ground, and exiled the remaining inhabitants. For all intents and purposes, Jewish sovereignty over the land of Israel had come to an end.

It seemed as though Jewish nationhood was over. That's the way it looked, at least, to everyone else. But someone forgot to tell the Jews.

And that's Haman's complaint. Here are the Jews, decades after being conquered and exiled from Israel. They are scattered all over the place and have no land to call their own. But somehow, they have the audacity to maintain laws of their own. They act as if they were still a self-respecting people among the family of nations. Don't they get it? *Give it up, already; it's over.* Get used to it, assimilate, disappear into your host culture – act like anyone else who's been conquered and dispersed.

We Persians, the new world power, have graciously taken in these Jewish exiles, these refugees from conquered Israel and Judah. We did so as a humanitarian gesture; we are a benevolent empire. We willingly provide for poor, unfortunate refugees. But all this only works if the refugees keep their part of the bargain. A refugee needs to understand he's a refugee. But these Jews just don't get it. They have the gall to come here to Persia, scatter everywhere, and hang onto their laws, pretending to maintain their status, somehow, as a sovereign nation. They are a paradox, a living oxymoron – a nation scattered among other nations.

Plus, they don't even keep the king's laws. All the other nations in the empire might have their own laws – their own provincial statutes, as it were – but they *also* have allegiance to the crown, and keep the king's laws too. But not the Jews – or, at least, not Mordecai. *If the king says you've got to bow whenever I come out in my motorcade, well, you've got to bow. But these landless Jews, they won't bow.* They don't hold up their end of the bargain; they don't play their parts, acting like good, docile refugees. They live here in Persia by virtue of our goodwill, but seem to exist in their own, deluded reality as a separate nation. *It's just not worth it for the king to keep them around…*

MOTHER PERSIA, OR QUEEN OF THE DELUSIONAL REFUGEES?

That's the argument Haman made to Ahasuerus when he first proposed doing away with the Jews. And now, months later, at Esther's banquet – while the king paces in the garden – everything once again rides on that argument, and on whether Haman can breathe life back into it.

Haman is in a difficult spot, but not an impossible one. If he can once again portray the Jews as a deluded band of refugees, he can still turn the tables. He can try to drive a wedge between Esther and her people, and make it extraordinarily difficult for Esther to champion their cause.

The king has left the room. Haman is now alone with Esther. To grasp the strength of Haman's position, let's play a mind game of sorts and imagine what arguments were available to Haman, even at this late moment. Let's reconstruct the nightmare scenario. What could he have said to Esther?

I would have said something like this: *Oh, Esther, I can't believe it. You were a Jew all this time? What an incredible misunderstanding. Imagine, our very own queen was once one of those poor, disheveled refugees from Palestine! It's amazing, almost funny; an "only in Persia" rags-to-riches story…* Haman would go on to explain to Esther that he never had anything against her personally, and that she, her friends, and her family have nothing to fear. They are entirely safe; she can shelter them in the palace. He would apologize for the mix-up about her Jewishness and her apparent inclusion in his decree of destruction, but then he would take care to point out the obvious: *Please, Esther, this whole idea that I was somehow out to get you, that you were ever personally endangered by me – it's so overblown. I never knew about your secret identity; none of us knew. How could we? And if we did, of course we would have spared you. You know, Esther, to be perfectly frank, I do think you need to take at least some responsibility for the miscommunication here. After all, Esther, it's not like you were so very up-front with the fact that you were a Jew this whole time…*

The key, of course, would be to try to separate Esther's destiny from that of the people she is trying to defend: *Look, Esther, you're our queen; you're not like the rest of those lawbreakers, the Jews. In a minute, the king is going to walk back in. I'll explain the whole misunderstanding; I'm good at that. We'll let him know that no one was trying to hurt you.… As for your former compatriots, the Jews – well, what has to happen to them is certainly unfortunate, but sometimes the good of the empire demands some painful sacrifices. Surely you, our queen, know that better than anyone. So please, Esther, let it go. Let the wheels of justice turn. And whatever you do, please don't cast your lot with those miserable refugees and their pitiful national aspirations. I'm saying this for your own sake, Esther. After all, you are Mother Persia. You don't want the king to start thinking, "Whose queen is she – ours, or theirs?"* If you were Esther, just how uncomfortable would you feel now?

TO CONQUER THE QUEEN

Let's return from our musings about Haman's arguments – what he might have said to Esther, alone in that room – and pick up the trail of the actual story the Megilla tells. The king returns to the banquet hall, and at that moment something happens that dramatically turns the tide. We don't know what Haman said to Esther, but we do know that he made one crucial mistake: when the king comes back, Haman is lying on Esther's couch.

> The king returned from the garden to the banquet hall, and Haman had fallen on the couch upon which Esther was

> [seated]. The king declared: "So, you would even conquer the queen while I am yet in the house!" The words [just] came out of the king's mouth, and they covered Haman's face. (Est. 7:8)

Ahasuerus boldly and suddenly accuses Haman of trying to seduce his wife while he is still in the house. At first, the king's accusation seems utterly preposterous. After everything Esther has told him, does he really think Haman is trying to seduce her? Hasn't Esther made it clear that Haman is her mortal enemy, that she despises him, wants him dead, and that the feeling is probably mutual? Has Ahasuerus somehow missed this rather unsubtle point?

The text of the Megilla nudges us in the direction of an answer. Right after the king's startling words about seducing the queen, the narrator adds the phrase "the words [just] came out of the king's mouth." What does this phrase add? Obviously, the words came out of the king's mouth – how else does anyone say anything? But the sense of the text is that the words just slipped out, without the king even consciously thinking about what he was saying. It is almost as if the king himself is shocked by what he has just said. Had Ahasuerus stopped to think, he would never have said what he did. But he spoke without thinking. When you speak without thinking, your rational mind is in abeyance, and your subconscious mind, your imaginings, do the talking.

For an entire day, the king had wondered whether Haman was romantically involved with his wife. At the banquet, Esther suddenly suggested otherwise: he wanted to kill her. But as we noted earlier, she did not contradict the king's fears; she actually *affirmed* the general direction of the king's suspicion: *He's trying to take me away from you.* Now that the king sees Haman on the couch, the old form of his suspicion returns, and as absurd as it may seem, he accuses Haman of seducing his wife. In the end, for the king, it's all the same: *He's trying to take her away from me.*

In a subtle way, the text makes this confusion evident in the king's choice of words. When the king declares that Haman is trying to seduce her while he's still in the house, the verb he uses is *lichvosh*, typically a military term that literally means "to conquer." The euphemism Ahasuerus chooses for his fantastical suspicion of marital infidelity is borrowed from the very real threat that Haman *does* pose: that he might kill and conquer both the queen and her people. It all makes perfect sense – if not to the rational mind, then to the irrational one. To the rational mind, once Esther reveals that Haman is trying to kill her, Haman on the couch with her means nothing. But to the irrational mind, to the subconscious mind – when the words just slip right out – Haman on the couch means everything. *I was right all along. He is trying to conquer her.*

HAMAN'S BACKYARD GALLOWS

The final blow for Haman comes when an obscure courtier, a man by the name of Harvonah, shows up and reveals a handy bit of information to the king. Harvonah's revelation could not have come at a better time:

> Then Harvonah, one of the king's eunuchs, declared before the king: "Also, there's a gallows that Haman made for Mordecai – the one who spoke loyally about the king – and [the gallows] is standing, fifty cubits tall, in Haman's yard." So the king said: "Hang him on it!" (Est. 7:9)

As we've seen, Haman built the gallows in a frenzied, obsessed attempt to kill Mordecai the very next morning, whatever the cost. In so doing, we suggested, Haman undercut the rationale he had so carefully constructed for his pogrom against the Jews. Remember: Haman had taken great pains to hide his personal grudge against Mordecai. When Mordecai initially wouldn't bow to him, Haman was infuriated, but he held himself back from ordering Mordecai killed. In the words of the Megilla, it was too petty in Haman's eyes to take vengeance against one man who refused to bow to him. Haman was above that – or was supposed to be. So instead, Haman constructed an elaborate plot to wipe out the entire nation of which Mordecai was a part. And to support it, Haman constructed an elegant rationale for why killing the Jews was right and just, behind which he could easily hide his personal animosities.

It was a well-crafted plan. But Haman failed to cover his tracks entirely. In his zeal to do away with Mordecai when he once again refused to bow to him, Haman gave in. He erected a gallows in his backyard. As we saw earlier, Haman never had a chance to ask the king's permission to hang Mordecai. But the gallows in the backyard remained standing, and its continued existence bore silent testimony to the bald truth that, in the end, it was personal all along. The notion that the Jews were lawbreakers, that they were immigrants who didn't live up to the implied social contract under which Persia continued to tolerate them – all that was a sham. The gallows for Mordecai made it clear that this argument, whatever its merit, was a mere pretext, not the true reason for Haman's pogrom against the Jews. The gallows in Haman's backyard attested to this, for anyone who bothered to look.

Until Haman's downfall was nearly assured, no one *did* bother to look. But now, as things began to fall apart for Haman, that changed. A courtier by the name of Harvonah took the liberty of informing the king about Haman's gallows – gallows that had been erected specifically with one victim in mind: Mordecai. Which Mordecai? As Harvonah so helpfully adds, "Mordecai, the one who spoke loyally about the king."

The last shred of respectability behind which Haman could hide now falls away. It's clear now: it's personal. Harvonah, moreover, shows that Haman was not out to kill just anybody. He was out to do away with Mordecai, the man who had foiled a plot to assassinate the king, the man whose loyalty to the king could not be questioned. Harvonah makes the choice for the king very stark: *Whose side are you on, sire? Who are your friends, and who are your enemies? Haman may have seemed loyal in the past, but look who he's trying to kill. He's trying to murder the one person you* know *has been loyal to you.*

AN INCONVENIENT TRUTH

That's enough for the king, and with a wave of his hand, Ahasuerus declares that Haman should be taken away, hanged on the very gallows he had prepared for Mordecai. It is undoubtedly a sweet moment for Esther. Her nemesis – and the mortal enemy of her people – is undone. Once Haman is dead, the king puts the finishing touch on the celebrations by bestowing gifts upon Esther and Mordecai. Everyone is smiling, and all looks wonderful. One would expect that in a few verses, the Megilla would draw to a close. But there are still three chapters of the Megilla left to go. Evidently, the story is not yet over. Why not? Because there's still one little problem. It's an inconvenient fact, easily overlooked in the revelry surrounding Haman's hanging, and in the pomp and circumstance of the king's gifts to Mordecai and Esther: Haman might be dead, but his decree of genocide against the Jews is still alive and well. Whether Haman and his minions will still have the last laugh, whether Haman will yet celebrate the demise of the Jews, albeit from his grave – this is the question to which the rest of the Megilla now devotes itself.

Chapter Seven

The King and I

In the wake of Haman's death, the king elevates Mordecai to the royal court, hands over Haman's mansion to Esther, and grants Mordecai use of his coveted signet ring. But these gifts, while impressive, are achingly irrelevant. The one thing that really counts, the one thing that Esther and Mordecai really care about, is the one thing Ahasuerus does not give them. He does not reverse the decree legislating the destruction of the Jewish people.

In blithely ignoring the fate of the Jews, it is not evident that the king is acting out of a deep and abiding malice – although he certainly might be. It may just be that he is horrifyingly indifferent. At the very least, the Jews and their welfare rank low on his list of priorities. Yes, Esther did, in passing, mention a threat to the Jews of his realm. But in all the hullabaloo surrounding Haman's hanging, that threat has gone unaddressed. The prospect of the Jews' imminent demise has not managed to hold the king's attention.

Esther's gambit, then, for all its brilliance, has failed. Esther had tried to effect the Jews' salvation backhandedly. She had emphasized to the king how Haman's decree threatened her own life, hoping that, in linking her fate to the fate of her people, she could save them both. She had hoped that in a single act of fury, the king would kill Haman and reverse his decree, saving her by annulling the edict that threatened her.

Alas, things didn't work out that way. In the words of the Megilla, "they hanged Haman and the king's anger abated" (Est. 7:10). In the end, the king's fury was spent in the mere act of killing Haman; he felt no compelling urge to go further. The king had taken a more conservative approach to assuring Esther's safety: he would, of course, safeguard his queen, but he felt no particular need to reverse any preexisting legislation. The day after Esther's carefully plotted wine feast with Haman and the king, the planned pogrom against the Jews lingered like a bad hangover.

In retrospect, the king's course of action, though regrettable, was almost to be expected. In responding to Esther's revelations about Haman, Ahasuerus had sought to take care of his own and do away with his personal enemies. Haman, who seems to have been after Ahasuerus's wife, if not his crown, has been disposed of. Mordecai, who had shown himself to be loyal, has been rewarded. And Esther, his queen, is safe. From the king's standpoint, what more is there to be done? In rewarding Mordecai with the trappings of power and a position in the court, he can rest assured that he's amply repaid those loyal to him. Now he can let the whole sordid affair involving Haman recede into the past and move on to happier things.

NO CARDS LEFT

Esther has played her hand, and still has not achieved her true aim. She now faces a grim choice. She must either accept that she has failed and retire to the safety of the palace, where she can shield Mordecai and perhaps a cohort of family and compatriots from the coming horror. Or she must go to the king with nothing but the unvarnished truth. If she is to cancel Haman's decree now, she must do so without the benefit of subterfuge. She must make a direct appeal to the king – not for her own life, which the king has already graciously granted – but for the lives of her people. She must beg him for their safety. And she must do this despite the considerable risk both to herself and to them.

Esther takes the leap. She shuns the safety of the palace and decides, once more, to go to the king. Here is the Megilla's account of that encounter:

> So again, Esther went to speak before the king. She fell at his feet, cried, and beseeched him to revoke the evil of Haman the Agagite, the plots he had plotted against the Jews. The king lifted his scepter and Esther got up and stood before the king. (Est. 8:3–4)

Now Esther cries. We asked earlier why, of all possible occasions in the Megilla, Esther would lose her composure and dissolve into tears at this particular moment. Hasn't the battle more or less been won? Hasn't the king shown himself to be on the Jews' side by deciding to kill Haman? But the answer should now be evident. It is precisely now – now that Haman is dead – that Esther is most vulnerable. Indeed, as far as Esther is concerned, this is the most dangerous moment she's yet experienced.[1]

While Haman was alive, Esther had found a way – albeit a dangerous way – to fight for her countrymen while gracefully

1. As if to emphasize the danger, the Megilla adds one more detail to the picture: the king lifts his scepter so Esther can approach him. The scene evokes an earlier moment in the Megilla. The last time the king lifted his scepter for Esther, he might, by law, have killed her instead for having entered unannounced. It seems we are witnessing a replay of that situation. The king's lifting of his scepter seems to underscore the danger of the moment. As if the content of Esther's request weren't dangerous enough, it appears that the king is back in his private chambers – so she is once more taking her life in her hands by approaching him.

keeping her own true allegiances out of the limelight. But now Haman is dead, and suddenly there is no more hiding. The woman whom the king views first and foremost as his queen, as Mother Persia, the feminine embodiment of his empire, will now openly declare her allegiance to another people, the Jews, and plead with the king to save them. What else can she do? To call this risky would be to understate the danger to an extreme. Having been granted permission to speak, Esther makes her plea:

> And she said: "If the king finds it pleasing, and if I have found favor before him, if the thing [I propose] seems fitting to the king, and if I am pleasing in his eyes, let [a decree] be written to rescind the letters [carrying] the plots of Haman … for how can I possibly bear to see the terrible [fate] that will befall my people? How can I possibly bear to see the destruction of those from whom I was born?" (Est. 8:5–6)

The queen passionately advocates on behalf of her people, making clear the depth of her feelings for her countrymen. In moving language, she tells the king how tormented she would be to watch her people's destruction from the safety of the palace. Implicitly, in the very act of making her plea, she has left behind this safety. She has revealed her true allegiances and cast her lot with the Jews, come what may.

A MALEVOLENT MAGNANIMITY

How does the king react? Does he give her what she wants? As one first reads the king's words, the answer is not immediately clear:

> And King Ahasuerus said to Esther the queen and to Mordecai the Jew: "Here, I have already given the House of Haman to Esther, and I've hanged him upon the gallows because he

> sought to harm the Jews. As for you, write what you like in the name of the king concerning the Jews, and seal it with the king's seal – because documents written in the name of the king and sealed with the king's seal cannot possibly be repealed." (Est. 8:7–8)

There king's response is vague. He doesn't categorically say yes or no. He hasn't really answered Esther's question directly, and it seems hard to pin down just what he is saying. But let's try.

Before addressing Esther's request, the king takes care to tick off a list of favors he has already granted: Here, I've already given you the House of Haman and have had him hanged because he threatened your friends, the Jews ... Is the king annoyed? Does he feel he's already done enough for Esther? With that kind of beginning, you almost expect him to continue: Now, what more could you want? Leave me alone already. Instead, the king becomes surprisingly magnanimous. He tells Mordecai and Esther that he is giving them license to use the king's signet ring, that they can write and sign whatever they want concerning the Jews. Great news, right? Not only that, he concludes by telling them just how powerful a gift this is:

> Documents written in the name of the king and sealed with the king's seal cannot possibly be repealed.

Well, what could be better? Esther and Mordecai have a free hand. The king has given them the ultimate carte blanche: permission to use his signet ring to sign into law anything they want concerning the Jews. What an unexpected bout of good fortune. Look at that Ahasuerus – what a swell guy! But then, just as you're breaking out the champagne, you begin to reconsider the meaning of what the king said. You add up all the pieces: Esther asked Ahasuerus to repeal Haman's decree. And somehow, for all the king's sudden and abundant generosity, he never directly said yes; he never told her he would repeal it. But that's a triviality, surely? He told Esther and Mordecai that they had carte blanche, that they could write whatever they wanted concerning the Jews. So that's all that matters, right? Why are you being so suspicious? But doubts still gnaw at you as you replay the king's last words in your mind: *"Documents written in the name of the king and sealed with the king's seal cannot possibly be repealed."*

And suddenly, the true import of the king's words hits you like a freight train. Ahasuerus's final phrase has a hair-raising double meaning. If decrees written and sealed by the crown truly can't be repealed, then that goes not just for whatever Esther and Mordecai might choose in the future to write concerning the Jews; *it goes for Haman's original decree too!*

The king has managed to give them everything and nothing at the same time. What good is the king's signet ring if you can't use it to reverse the decree of genocide against your people? Sure, write whatever you like concerning the Jews, but keep in mind: documents sealed with the king's seal are sacrosanct. Haman's decree will stand, no matter what.[2] Bottom line: the king has said no to

---

2. One of the ambiguities in the king's words to Esther centers on how one translates the crucial Hebrew word *ki*, linking the last two phrases in his reply: "As for you, write what you like concerning the Jews, and seal it with the king's seal [*ki*] documents written in the name of the king... cannot possibly be repealed" (Est. 8:8).

   We've been translating *ki* as "because," its usual translation. The word, however, can sometimes mean "but," and if it is being used in that sense here, it would change the tone – but not really the content – of Ahasuerus's words. In particular, translating *ki* as "but" would have Ahasuerus refer directly, rather than obliquely, to Haman's original decree. He would be saying something like this: Look, I've already rewarded you with Haman's estate and killed him. What more do you want? Write whatever you want concerning the Jews, but remember: documents [such as Haman's] that have been written and sealed in the name of the king can't be repealed. In this scenario, the king's annoyance shines through even more brightly. He directly refuses Esther's request for repeal, while suggesting self-righteously that he's already done as much as can be expected for her friends the Jews.

Esther. He has couched his refusal in ambiguous, self-righteous tones, but he has still said no. He has generously rewarded Esther and Mordecai with all sorts of gifts. Why does she want more than this? Lurking behind his words seems a kind of annoyance with her, a sense that she has pushed him too far. *I'd love to help, Esther, but my hands are tied. You know, we here in Persia are very serious about our laws. And sadly, by law, I can't revoke that unfortunate decree doing away with these newfound "countrymen" of yours, the Jews.* Ahasuerus claims his hands are tied. The law just can't be revoked. Maybe. But is he as powerless as he claims to be? Is there really nothing he could do? Or is he only too happy to allow the Jews to be slaughtered, and to see how his queen takes it when the "countrymen" she suddenly feels so strongly about are eliminated?

It seems like the end of the line. What is there left to try? Indeed, if the Megilla had ended here, and it were up to you to conjecture what happened to the Jews of the Persian Empire back in 480 BCE, you would have to guess that they were utterly destroyed.

But of course, the Jews weren't destroyed; the continued existence of Jews today is living testimony to that fact. So how did we survive, given the king's disastrous rebuff of Esther's eleventh-hour plea? Mordecai and Esther were in a seemingly impossible position. How did they get out of it?

Chapter Eight

War Games

After Esther's heroic, but failed, attempt to win the repeal of Haman's decree, she and Mordecai must face the reality that Haman's planned day of killing is here to stay. Whether the king can, in fact, overturn Haman's original decree is now beside the point. The king has made clear that he either can't or won't. Given this, is there anything that can be done other than hunker down and hope the end comes swiftly?

There *is* something that can still be done, but seeing it requires looking a paradox in the eye without flinching: Can Esther and Mordecai somehow undo Haman's decree without actually undoing it? Is there a way to leave the decree in place but still give the Jews a chance to survive?

Let's take stock of what Esther and Mordecai have to work with. What tools do they have at their disposal? Esther didn't get what she wanted from her audience with the king, but she did get some things she *didn't* want. She and Mordecai got permission to use the king's signet ring, and Mordecai was elevated to an important position in the king's court, with all the attendant trappings of power. Of course, none of this counts for much when the one thing you can't do is overturn the decree that would wipe out your people. Nevertheless, sometimes in life, you have to work with what you have.

So what *can* they do? Well, to start with, if you can't revoke Haman's decree, but you do have the king's signet ring, giving you power to "write what you want concerning the Jews," there is a next-best thing you could try: promulgating a counter-decree, a second decree that contradicts the first one.

KNOWING YOUR AUDIENCE

Conventional wisdom has it that Mordecai wrote legislation giving the Jews of the realm the right to defend themselves against Haman's legions. That's true, but it's not the whole truth. In fact, the right to defend themselves was only a very small part of the decree that Mordecai chose to issue:

> [Mordecai wrote] that the king had allowed the Jews in every city to gather themselves together, and to stand and defend their lives; to destroy, to slay, and cause to perish, all the forces… that would assault them. [The Jews could slay their enemy's] little ones and women, and take their [possessions as] spoils of war. (Est. 8:11)

Now let's think about this. I understand the Jews needing to defend themselves. But what's this about killing women and children? That sounds rather gratuitous. And taking spoils of war? The Jews are not out for bounty; they would be happy just to escape with their lives.[1] Why does Mordecai write all this? A clue comes from

1. As we noted earlier, the Jews, in the end, do not avail themselves of these rights. On the contrary, the Megilla goes out of its way, more than once, to state that, though

the audience for whom Mordecai is writing. To whom are these decrees addressed?

> [The king's scribes] wrote to the officials, the governors and princes of the provinces that are from India unto Ethiopia, one hundred twenty and seven provinces… (Est. 8:9)

The letters dispatched by Mordecai were addressed to every official, governor, and lieutenant governor in all the far-flung provinces of the Persian Empire. Mordecai's prime audience was not the Jews – the disorganized, puny forces who would be fighting to defend their lives – but the officials throughout the civilized world who controlled the far more powerful machinery of state, the men throughout Ahasuerus's realm who controlled the provincial armies, the police, and the fire departments.

Indeed, in any pogrom, the balance of power resides not so much in the match-up between the actual combatants as in the silent role played by officialdom. The question is not really whether the Jews can try to defend themselves if they like. Jews can always *try* to defend themselves – even during the Crusades, even on Kristallnacht. A lot of good it's going to do them. The question is: What is the position of the state? What will the police and fire departments do when the mobs start to converge? Will they stand on the sidelines, giving their silent assent while Jewish houses and businesses burn? Or will they intervene to stop the violence? The only thing that really counts here is where the sympathies of the governors and local officials lie.

Mordecai's decrees are aimed straight at these people. He must win over their hearts and minds. Or, more precisely, he must

---

victorious, the Jews made sure not to take any bounty from their enemies. It would seem that the Jews never had any intention, or interest, in taking spoils of war. So why does Mordecai authorize it?

appeal to their sense of political self-preservation. More than any physical battle, Mordecai is engaged in a war of public relations – and everything he does is calculated to win it.

HAS THE PALACE GONE MAD?

The dictates of public relations explain why Mordecai does not limit himself to giving the Jews license to defend themselves. He must go beyond this, well beyond it. Here's why: Put yourself in the shoes of an ambitious lieutenant governor of Turkmenistan. Several months ago, you received an official letter of state, bearing the king's seal and legislating the murder of all the Jews in your province on a single, blood-soaked day. Since then, you've been gearing up for the occasion: putting local antisemites in touch with each other, lending office space to militias, deregulating the small arms market, you name it. Then, one fine day, a royal messenger shows up at the governor's mansion with another letter of state. You open it, only to find that it is a decree in favor of the Jews. The Jews are being given the right to defend themselves during the very day of killing for which you have been so assiduously preparing.

How would you react? You'd think the palace had gone mad. What is the king thinking? Taken together, the two decrees have, in effect, legislated a day of civil war. The blue team will attack the red team, and everyone on the red team should fight back as best they can. What is this, color war? These are human lives we're talking about; it's not a game.

Mordecai knows that whatever decree he promulgates in the name of the king will be weighed against a first decree that still remains in force, Haman's decree of genocide. Every provincial governor throughout the empire will have a decision to make. They will have to make sense of a senseless situation and figure out how to act in the face of two decrees pointing in diametrically opposite directions. It is 480 BCE, and there is no email, no telephone line available to check on the palace's true intentions. The governors will seek clues, anything that will help them determine which decree, if either, represents the real position of the palace on the matter of the Jews.

The first decree, Haman's edict legislating death to all the Jews, had been formulated in the harshest, most gratuitously violent language imaginable. It had given license "to destroy, to slay, and cause to perish all the Jews, from young to old, little ones and women... and to plunder their possessions" (Est. 3:13). Mordecai knows that if the Jews are to have any chance at all, his second decree must go toe-to-toe with the first. It cannot state, vaguely, that the Jews may defend themselves as best they can. Provincial governors throughout the land would weigh the two decrees and find the first more forceful, more specific – and therefore more convincing – than the second. They would conclude that Haman's edict represented the real mindset of the king, while the second decree was mere window dressing, issued simply to appease some political interest or another.

Mordecai's second decree, then, needs to be every bit as violent, every bit as bloodthirsty, as the first. It is not enough to allow the Jews to defend themselves. They must be encouraged to take offensive action; they must be given license to launch a preemptive strike. If Haman and his minions had been granted permission to kill man, woman, and child, Mordecai must now see to it that his decree gives the same license to the Jews. If Haman's militias had been granted permission to despoil the Jews of their possessions, the Jews must now be given the right to do the same. Do the Jews care about these financial perks? Do they have the slightest intention of taking their enemies' possessions? No, it's the furthest thing from their minds. As the Megilla states time and again, when the war came, the Jews took no spoils. But Mordecai's decree has nothing to do with what's actually going to happen. It's about appearances, and appearances only.

A PARADE BEFORE ITS TIME

Yet even Mordecai's provocatively-worded edict cannot, in itself, guarantee the safety of his people. At best, even if Mordecai's letters perfectly match the pitch, tone, and wording of Haman's, the most they can do is provide an equal counterweight to Haman's decree. The Jews' chances are still no better than fifty-fifty. Some governors may decide to take the second decree more seriously than the first; others may presume that the first decree is the one they are best advised to listen to. In the end, all Mordecai's decree can do is create confusion about the king's intentions. Something more is needed to tip the balance. All of this leads us to understand something else Mordecai does. The Megilla goes out of its way to record a celebratory parade through the streets of Shushan. Mordecai struts through the streets of the city's Jewish quarter wearing his royal finest, while all the assembled crowds deliriously proclaim their joy:

> And Mordecai went out from before the king in royal dress, wearing turquoise and white robes, with a big golden crown... and the city of Shushan erupted in happiness. (Est. 8:15)

Now, if you didn't have a scroll of Esther handy, and you had to guess when that celebration took place, what would you say? Would you guess that the parade happened *before* or *after* the Jews emerged victorious from the battle against their enemies? I think most of us would have guessed *afterward*. A ticker-tape parade only makes sense when it celebrates victory. Before you win, what is there to celebrate? If the battle yet looms, why would everyone be so happy?

But the chronology of the Megilla makes absolutely clear that the parade came *before* the war. Here the Jews are, tensely preparing for an epic battle in which the lives of their women and children hang in the balance, and they have the time and interest to throw a parade for Mordecai? Are they mad? They should be cleaning their guns and stockpiling their buckshot.

But on second thought, it makes perfect sense. You would celebrate before you win only if you were so confident of victory that defeat was unthinkable. You would celebrate before you win only if you didn't mind projecting an attitude of untrammeled arrogance to the watching world.

And that's precisely what Mordecai wants to do. The parade is not a vain attempt at self-congratulation; it is a calculated spectacle designed for a very particular audience: midlevel officials throughout Ahasuerus's empire. The celebration is a charade. It's all part of a psychological warfare campaign. If you were a lieutenant governor in Turkmenistan, and you were weighing which of the two conflicting decrees in your hands represented the true position of the palace, what message would you take from the news that the Jews were celebrating in Shushan, and Mordecai was parading through the streets in royal robes? *My goodness, how the tides have changed! I guess the palace is behind the Jews after all.*

If you are a Persian governor with your finger on the pulse of the empire, who are you going to support now?

The parade ups the ante. If Mordecai's decree created a good, solid sense of confusion over whom the palace supports, his parade is an attempt to tip the scales of public perception decisively in favor of the Jews. Mordecai has used the tools available to him – the king's signet ring and his royal clothes – to build the illusion that the palace backs the Jews. The reality, of course, is emphatically otherwise. The king is at best indifferent to the peril facing the Jews, and at worst, he is a behind-the-scenes facilitator. Mordecai is staking everything on a grand bluff. But all else has failed, and at this point, it's the only chance his people have.

THE TIDE TURNS

Some otherwise inexplicable things now start to come into focus. The Megilla records that in the wake of Mordecai's parade, people – regular, everyday Persians – started converting to Judaism, because fear of the Jews had begun to settle on them (Est. 8:17). It also tells us that Mordecai's fame and reputation grew throughout the empire (Est. 9:4). Now, why tell us these things? When the Jews' lives are on the line, who cares about Mordecai's fame, and who cares about converts? These developments are barometers of public perception. They indicate that in the minds of everyday Persians, and in the minds of the officials who represented them, the fortunes of the Jews were rising ever higher. And because of the success of these public relations efforts, because of these changed perceptions, when the fated day of the pogrom finally arrived, the tide had at last turned:

> The Jews gathered in all their cities to take offensive action against all who would cause them harm; and no one stood in their way, for their fear had fallen upon all the nations. And all the officers of the nations and governors and potentates elevated the Jews, for the fear of Mordecai had fallen upon them. (Est. 9:2–3)

The governors and potentates now rally behind the Jews rather than facilitate their extermination. The firefighters and police have become allies of the Jews rather than silent accomplices in their demise. Given this turn of events, the Jews manage a turnabout in their fortunes, and on the day they were slated to be destroyed, they gain the upper hand against their enemies. Finally, the Jews appear to be safe. Mordecai's carefully crafted illusion seems to have achieved its design.

But wait. The Megilla is still not finished telling its story. One thing stands between the Jews and a happy ending. There is still one force that can stop the Jews' momentum, one person who can still shatter the illusion that the king backs the Jews – and that person is the king himself.

THE FINAL HURDLE

There is one last moment of truth in the Megilla, when everything can still go badly wrong. Late in the day on the thirteenth of Adar, after it has become clear that the Jews have intimidated their enemies and held their own against them, a report on the fighting reaches the king:

> That day, the number of those killed in Shushan, the capital, was brought before the king. And the king said to Esther the queen: "In Shushan, the capital, the Jews killed and obliterated five hundred souls, aside from the ten sons of Haman. Who knows what they've done in the other provinces of the empire? And now, [Esther,] what is your request? It will be given to you. What is your entreaty? It shall be done." (Est. 9:11–12)

The king's promise of aid to Esther is not new. Several times already, the king has asked Esther what she wanted, and several times already, he has promised to give to her what she asked for: once when Esther first approached him in his private chambers, and again when he granted her license to speak at the banquet attended by the king and Haman. Indeed, then as now, he used the same, formulaic expression: "What is your request? It will be given to you. What is your entreaty? It shall be done." Yet now there is a difference. If you look carefully at the text, you will find that each and every one of those earlier times, the king said even more. He always told Esther: "What is your entreaty? Up to half the kingdom, and it will be done." This time, though, this last time, he leaves out that extra phrase. Now, he no longer promises her half the kingdom should she ask for it. Gone is the air of largesse and chivalry that accompanied his earlier vows to do her bidding. He will act on her desires, but he seems to make this promise through gritted teeth.

Why has the king's patience suddenly worn so thin? The first part of the verse tells us: "That day, the number of those killed in Shushan, the capital, was brought before the king." The king has seen just about as much of Jewish vigilantism as he is willing to take. *Look, Esther, your Jewish friends have already killed five hundred loyal Persian citizens – and that's in Shushan alone. God only knows what they've done in the other provinces. Now, is that enough for you, or do you still want something else?* The king seems to be suggesting that the killing has gone on long enough; can't we call an end to this madness now?

WHAT STOPPING NOW WOULD MEAN

We are so used to reading the Purim story that it's not easy to see how it could have ended differently. What, indeed, would have happened if the palace had called a halt to the war right then, barring further Jewish use of arms? What if the king had issued an edict demanding that the Jews put aside their weapons and stand down, twenty-four hours after the beginning of hostilities? Such an edict would have been disastrous, for although the Jews have the upper hand, the war isn't over yet. There are still skirmishes taking place throughout the empire. A third declaration in the name of the king would immediately reverse the hard-won perception that the Jews enjoyed the blessing of the palace. The lieutenant governors of provinces, still holding two contradictory decrees in their hands – Haman's original decree and Mordecai's counter-decree – would see in this new, third edict a statement of the *real* sympathies of the king. *I guess that first decree was the primary one all along...* Such a declaration would bring the hordes of Jew-haters out of the woodwork. Licking their wounds, they would see in this third decree renewed license to finish off their enemies.

BET YOUR BOTTOM DOLLAR ON TOMORROW

The king offers Esther tenuous support, at best. How does Esther respond? She knows she cannot ask for too much; there are limits to how far she can press him. So she replies carefully, asking for only two small things:

> If it pleases the king, give tomorrow to the Jews of Shushan to continue what they've done today, and let the ten sons of Haman be hanged upon the gallows. (Est. 9:13)

Esther stakes everything on one last gamble. She asks the king to wait just one more day before ending the Jews' right to use arms. And she asks for one more little thing: take the sons of Haman – already dead – and hang them on a tree.

What does Esther have in mind? Why hang people who are already dead? How many times can you kill them? What Esther cares about is appearances. She makes one last, bold effort to ensure that Mordecai's grand bluff does not unravel. She wants the dead bodies of Haman's sons to be seen by all, swinging in the wind on the royal gallows. She wants a final, graphic reminder to all enemies of the Jews that the royal family stands behind the events of the past day. She is looking for a symbol to intimidate the enemies of the Jews into standing down, something dramatic that will indicate to them that the Jews cannot be challenged further. Ironically, the very bodies of Haman's progeny will become Esther's final weapon.

In acting as she does, Esther puts the final touches on a grand deception. She has made it seem as if the palace is unwavering in its support of the Jews. No one knows that all the Jews have is one more day. No one knows that at the stroke of midnight, all their royal carriages will turn back into humble pumpkins.

Luckily, that one extra day turns out to be enough. In the provinces, the enemies of the Jews stood down after the first twenty-four hours. In Shushan, the battle continued into the next day; but then, in the final hours of that extra day, the last of the antisemites laid down their arms, giving in to the perception of invincibility manufactured by Mordecai and Esther. If the conflict had gone on a little longer, everything might have been different. The true intentions of Ahasuerus might have come out, and there might have been no Purim to celebrate after all. But as it was, the victory – and the bluff that gave rise to it – was complete, just in the nick of time. All's well that ends well, and in the giddy celebrations that follow, there is much gift giving and revelry. But before we leave the story of the Megilla behind, let's consider a question we raised earlier but didn't answer: the question of Purim's name.

WHAT'S IN A NAME?

As we all know, the name of Purim derives from the lots (*pur*) that Haman cast to determine the day on which he would exterminate us. But, as we noticed before, in the beginning of this book, this name is strange indeed: why should we name our holiday after *that*? I could understand calling it Esther Day or Mordecai Day, even Victory in Persia Day – but why *Purim*, of all things? Why enshrine the instrument of chance selected by our nemesis to do away with us? We raised this concern earlier, and it is now time to address it. The name "Purim," we shall discover, contains an astounding hidden meaning, a meaning that will deepen our understanding of the events of Purim and their spiritual significance. This new view of the name "Purim" is now accessible to us, for the questions we've been struggling with have primed us to be able to discern it. Let us turn our gaze to this question about Purim's name, and see what we are able to find.

Part II

Purim: Lots and Vows

Chapter Nine

But Why Call It Purim?

For clarity about the meaning of Purim's name, the logical place to look is the Book of Esther, the biblical book that records the events of Purim. Fortunately for us, that scroll – the Megilla – does contain an explanation of why the day is called "Purim." Unfortunately, the explanation is fraught with difficulty. Let's take a moment to see what it says.

THE CASE OF THE MIXED-UP VERSES

The Megilla's explanation of Purim's name comes toward the middle of its ninth chapter, which records the process by which Purim was formalized as a holiday. It was first celebrated spontaneously by the Jews whose lives were actually saved. Later, through a series of decrees promulgated by Mordecai and Esther, it grew into an actual, legislated holiday that would be observed year after year by Jews around the globe. Right in the middle of recounting that formalization process, the Megilla takes a break, and begins a three-sentence digression on why Purim is known as "Purim."

> For Haman the son of Hammedata, the Agagite, the enemy of all the Jews, had plotted against the Jews to destroy them, and had cast "pur," that is, the lot, to terrify them, and to destroy them. But when [Esther] came before the king, [the king] commanded by means of letters that [Haman's] wicked thoughts, which he had devised against the Jews, should recoil upon his own head, and he and his sons were hanged on the gallows. That's why they called these days "Purim." (Est. 9:24–26)

If you examine these verses, you'll notice that their order seems wrong. The first verse tells us that Haman tried to kill us, and he cast lots to find a day on which to do so. The second tells us that, luckily, Esther managed to save us. And the third tells us "that's why the holiday is called 'lots.'" But *what* is why? Saying "that's why" implies that you are referring back to the last thing that was said. But the immediately preceding idea is that Esther saved us, not that Haman cast lots! Something seems out of place here.

If you rearranged the ideas by, say, flipping the order of the last two verses, things would seem to make more sense: Haman tried to kill us and he cast lots – which, by the way, is why they call the holiday lots – but luckily, Esther managed to save us. There, that seems to make better sense. But that's not the way the Megilla has it. The Megilla says, in effect: Haman tried to kill us, Esther saved us… and that's why they called the holiday "lots." How are we to make sense of this?

Actually, the verses make perfect sense as they are written, but we'll have to work to understand them. In particular, we'll soon see that these verses contain an elaborate double entendre; they have two meanings. In one, the holiday is named "Purim" after Haman's lots, as we assumed earlier. But the Megilla seems to be hinting at an alternate meaning as well, in which the holiday is not named after Haman's lots. In this second meaning, the holiday is named not for what Haman did, but for what Esther did when she went before the king. In this second meaning, the very name "Purim" means something entirely different from what we've grown up to think it means.

We will explore these ideas further in a moment. For now, suffice it to say that the ninth chapter of the Megilla points obliquely to a whole new way of looking at Purim. If we follow its lead, it emerges that the name "Purim" reflects not the caprice of our enemy, but an unseen facet of the designs of our heroine.

WHY CAN'T ESTHER BOW OUT?

In order to unravel the mystery behind Purim's name, we need to look more carefully at the queen we thought we knew. We will find an important clue if we return to Esther's first moment of truth, her earliest recorded exchange with Mordecai, when the hesitant queen initially agreed to risk her life by invading the king's private chambers to plead for her people.

Let's go back to that moment and replay those events. Mordecai told Esther that whether she acted or not, he was confident that the Jews would survive: "If you keep silent at this time, salvation will come to the Jews from somewhere else" (Est. 4:14). But he also told her that she must act. If she should remain silent, it would be a disaster not for the Jews – they would come out fine – but for *her*: "If you keep silent at this time, salvation will come to the Jews from somewhere else, but you and your father's house will be destroyed"(Est. 4:14).

We were puzzled, earlier, by Mordecai's position. Esther, as we established earlier, faced a terrible risk in going to the king. She risked destroying her image as "Mother Persia" and endangered her life. So if Mordecai was *really* so confident about the Jews' chances, even without Esther's intervention – why did Esther have to act? Maybe the rational thing was for Esther simply to bow out and let that alternative scenario take its course. Why did Esther have to walk the plank? We raised these questions earlier. It is time now to try and answer them.

WHERE HAVE WE HEARD THESE WORDS BEFORE?

The key to understanding what Mordecai tells Esther lies in a surprising fact: we've heard these words before. Mordecai, when he tells all this to Esther, is actually quoting words written centuries earlier, before Ahasuerus's kingdom was even a gleam in the eye of history. Uncanny hallmarks of Mordecai's speech – its broad theme, its literary signature, even its very words and phrases – can be discerned in the Torah itself, in a passage tucked away in an inconspicuous corner of the book of Numbers. Is this a coincidence? Maybe. But let's take a look at some of the striking similarities between these two passages:

A *Na'ara*

The Megilla describes Esther – the person Mordecai is speaking to – as a *na'ara,* the Hebrew term for a girl on the cusp of adulthood. Likewise, the section of Numbers that I am talking about concerns itself with laws pertaining to just such a girl, a *na'ara.*

A Married Girl

Esther, the *na'ara,* is taken by Ahasuerus as his wife. The *na'ara* in Numbers also marries.

Guidance Concerning Relationship with a Spouse

Mordecai tells Esther how she must act toward Ahasuerus. Likewise, the passage in Numbers gives laws that govern the relationship between a *na'ara* and her husband.

In Her Father's house

Mordecai tells the *na'ara* [Esther] that she is risking her own destruction and the destruction of "her father's house." As it turns out, he got this phrase from somewhere. Our "mystery passage" in the book of Numbers concludes with "These are the laws of a *na'ara* in her father's house."

Silence

Mordecai warns Esther about how disastrous it would be for her to keep silent. Likewise, the passage in Numbers talks about the disastrous consequences of keeping silent.

A Short Window of Time

Mordecai suggests that Esther must break her silence *right now*. There is a sense of urgency in his words. Similarly, the passage in Numbers delimits a short period of time – a single day – in which silence must be broken to avert untoward results.

In a moment, I'll tell you which scriptural passage in the book of Numbers I'm talking about. But first, take note of one more link between Mordecai's speech and that passage in the book of Numbers. It has to do with the particular word for "silence" that Mordecai uses, and the distinctive way he employs that word.

Doubled Silence

The Hebrew language has more than one word for silence. One is the verb *lishtok*; the other, the verb *lehaḥarish*. When Mordecai tells Esther she cannot remain silent, he uses *lehaḥarish*. And if you read carefully, you'll notice that Mordecai uses the verb twice in rapid succession: *im haḥaresh taḥarishi* (Est. 4:14). The repetition is not, in and of itself, all that remarkable. The Torah does this now and then, using a verb twice in a row. The repetition generally serves to emphasize a point, to bring it home with finality.[1] What

1. Thus, when speaking of a crime that is a capital offense, the Torah will occasionally write *mot yumat*, "he shall die; yes, die." Some translations render this as "he will surely die." The idea, though, is the same: the double form of the verb connotes emphasis.

is remarkable is that *lehaḥarish* appears as a doubled verb in only one other place in the entire Hebrew Bible. Besides Mordecai's speech, the only other place where this happens is, you guessed it, in the book of Numbers, in the passage we've been talking about, the one that bears all the other hallmarks of Mordecai's speech.

So where *is* Mordecai quoting from? I'm glad you asked. Mordecai is hinting at the thirtieth chapter of the book of Numbers, which deals with one of the most obscure topics in the Bible, a process known as *hafarat nedarim,* "the annulment of vows." What is *hafarat nedarim,* and what does it have to do with Mordecai and Esther?

Chapter Ten

The Sound of Silence

According to the Torah, people may choose to take vows, thereby imposing certain restrictions upon themselves that would not otherwise encumber them (Num. 30:3). For example, someone might take a vow that "Joe's possessions are now forbidden to me." He would then be required by Torah law to abide by the vow and avoid benefiting from Joe's possessions. Now, in describing these laws, the Torah declares that sometimes a husband has the ability to annul his wife's vow. In particular, if a young girl, a *na'ara*, who is married takes a vow that would cause her to experience hardship – say, never again to eat certain healthful foods (see Rambam, *Hilkhot Nedarim* 12:3) – her husband may protest and thereby annul the vow.

There's a catch, though. He may annul the vow only on the day he first hears about it. If he waits to protest, he loses the right to annul, and the vow will stand, regardless of what he later says. Here is the language of the passage in Numbers that details these points:

> Any vow or restrictive oath that would cause hardship, her husband can affirm [the vow] or the husband can annul it. [But] if the husband is silent, yes, silent, from day to day, then he will have affirmed all her vows or restrictions. He has affirmed them, for he has been silent on the day he heard of them. And if [the husband later tries to] annul [her vow] after he [first] heard of it [and was silent], he bears her sin. These are the laws of a [*na'ara*]...in her father's house.[1] (Num. 30:14–17)

As we've seen, Mordecai's speech is saturated with language borrowed from these laws of vows. He, too, speaks of a married *na'ara* "in her father's house," and of silence that must be broken quickly. He, too, uses this doubled form of the verb *lehaḥarish* (*im haḥaresh taḥarishi*). Why does Mordecai's speech so closely follow this passage? To find out, let's go back and examine more carefully the text in the book of Numbers.

THE THIRD OPTION

When a married woman takes a vow, "her husband can affirm [the vow] or her husband can annul it" (Num. 30:14).

When a woman takes a vow that imposes personal hardship upon herself, the Torah seems to give the husband two options: he can declare that he affirms his wife's vow, in which case it stands, or he can protest it, in which case it is annulled. The very next verse, though, seems to introduce us to a third option:

> "If her husband keeps silent, yes, silent."

1. The Torah speaks of the *na'ara* being in her "father's house" since she is just emerging from being a minor into adulthood. In the *na'ara* transition phase from childhood to adulthood, she remains under the jurisdiction of her father in certain legal respects.

What, exactly, is this third option all about? What stance is the husband taking by his silence, and how does the Torah relate to that? The language used for the husband's silence is, as we mentioned before, a doubled form of the word *lehaḥarish*. We've observed that the Hebrew language has at least two verbs for silence: *lishtok* and *lehaḥarish*. Why would a language have two words for the same idea? Well, probably because what looks like one idea is really two. Each word conveys a different shade of meaning. What, then, are the nuances of each word?

Let's talk about *lishtok* first. The word, as it is used in the Hebrew Bible, often describes the quiet of inanimate objects. For example, in the book of Jonah, when Jonah tells the sailors to throw him overboard, he counsels them that if they do so, *yishtok hayam* – "the sea will be silent from upon you" (Jonah 1:12); that is, the sea will be still, and will no longer threaten their lives. *Lishtok* means "to be still." Anyone or anything can be still. But there is another kind of silence that can be experienced only by human beings and not lifeless objects such as the sea. It is a type of silence denoted by the Hebrew verb *lehaḥarish*, a word used only for sentient beings. What, exactly, does *lehaḥarish* mean? The word *lehaḥarish* comes from the three-letter root Ḥ-R-SH.

As a noun, this string of letters denotes a deaf person. The verb form of the noun, *lehaḥarish*, would then seem to mean "to make oneself deaf," to act as if one has not heard. A sea is either still or it is astir. It does not put its fingers in its ears and make itself deaf. Only people do that.

This word *lehaḥarish* in the book of Numbers describes the husband's silence in the face of his wife's extremely discomfiting vow. The Torah, then, is saying that a man might do something other than affirming or annulling the vow. He might choose to make himself deaf to it. He might remain silent, as if he does not hear. In the face of his wife's impetuous vow to accept pain and suffering, he might choose to maintain an oblivious kind of neutrality. The remainder of the verse tells us how the Torah treats this neutrality:

> If the husband is silent, yes, silent, from day to day, then he will have affirmed all her vows or restrictions. He has affirmed them, for he has been silent on the day he heard of them. (Num. 30:15)

Silence, the Torah tells us, is tacit affirmation. The third option *looks* like an option, but it is illusory. The husband *did* hear his wife's vow, he is aware of the pain and hardship that faces her, and his silence is a choice too. Keeping quiet, staying out of the situation, the vain attempt to scramble for neutral ground, is also a choice. It is a choice to accept the vow.

YES, NO, AND MAYBE

It is all too easy to believe that for every question, there are three possible answers: yes, no, and maybe. Will it rain tomorrow? You might say yes; you might say no. Or you might profess ignorance and say, "Maybe; I just don't know." This last option, "maybe," is quite appealing. You don't know whether it's going to rain tomorrow, do you? So why bother committing yourself? It seems so much more logical just to admit you don't know and say maybe. Sometimes, though, "maybe" isn't an option.

Say, for example, a man shows up at his doctor's office one day for a routine physical, and the doctor comes back with worrying news: there's something suspicious about the x-ray. The doctor refers the man to a highly specialized oncologist, who diagnoses stage-three pancreatic cancer, which is almost always fatal. There's a bit of good news, though: a new, experimental treatment holds out hope for a cure. An aggressive regimen of chemotherapy may well save his life. He schedules an appointment for the following week to begin treatment.

In the meantime, the man seeks a second opinion. He consults with the only other living expert in the field, who surveys the situation and tells the patient that yes, he can see why the first specialist *thought* he had cancer, but in fact, he is perfectly fine, cancer free. Moreover, he'd better not take the experimental drugs – they are likely to kill him.

What should the man do? These are the only two specialists in the world who know anything about this form of cancer, and they have arrived at diametrically opposed diagnoses. Every fiber of his being pushes him to abstain, not to commit. *You don't know, so just sit this one out.* But the harsh reality is that there's no way to sit this one out. You either take the chemotherapy or you don't. There is no third option.

William James's book *The Will to Believe* makes the same point about belief in God. Believers say there is a God. Atheists say there isn't. And agnostics say they aren't sure. That last option sure *sounds* sensible. You can't touch God, you can't see Him – how can you know for sure one way or the other? Why not just remain neutral on the question?

James contends, however, that in real life, agnosticism is not a rational position. It is untenable. You have to live your life, and there are only two ways to live it: either you live your life reaching toward a Higher Being, or you don't. Those are really the only two options. There is no way to abstain.

It's that way with cancer, it's that way with God – and, the Torah says, it's that way with vows. If a man hears that his wife has taken an impetuous vow that puts her in a place of hardship, he has only two options before him: he can affirm her vow or protest it. He cannot play deaf. If he tries to adopt a position of neutrality and remains silent, he has taken a side. His silence is tantamount to assent. He has heard her vow, and he has tacitly affirmed it.

THE PRICE OF SILENCE

What are the consequences of silent affirmation? The Torah tells us at the end of the passage:

> If [the husband tries to] annul [her vow] after he [first] heard of it [and was silent], he bears her sin. (Num. 30:16)

If the husband, after remaining silent on the day he first heard of his wife's vow, later has second thoughts and wants to annul the vow, he can't. His wife's vow has already been affirmed through his tacit assent, and he has no power to annul it anymore (see Rashi to Numbers 30:16). Moreover, the Torah continues, if she subsequently fails to live up to the terms of the vow, it is he who bears her sin. Rashi is clear about what this means: although she is the one who didn't keep her vow, *he* is the one deemed to have sinned. Rashi explains why: "You see from here that someone who causes his friend to stumble [morally or spiritually] takes their place, as far as responsibility for the misdeed is concerned" (Rashi to Numbers 30:16).

CAN ESTHER ABSTAIN?

The passage in Numbers begins by stating *ishah yekimenu, ve'ishah yeferenu* – her husband can affirm it; her husband can annul it. But there's a double entendre in the verse, suggests Mordecai. *Ishah* doesn't just mean "her husband." Depending on the vowelization, the word can also mean "a woman."[2] *A woman. A woman can*

2. The Torah is written without vowelization; the vowels are implied. In the book of Numbers, *ishah* is spelled *alef, yod, shin, heh,* and is vowelized with a dot in the *heh.*

affirm; a woman can annul. Hundreds of years after this passage was written, Mordecai tells Esther that, in effect, these words are speaking to her. Yes, in the plain meaning of the verse, *ishah* means husband, and the text refers to a man's ability to annul his wife's vows; but it is as if there is a secondary, prophetic meaning to the text, in which *ishah* can be read as "woman." There will come a time when a woman will be in a position to annul her spouse's impetuous words, a declaration that would cause extreme hardship – and that moment, Mordecai tells Esther, is now.

It is as if Mordecai is reading that entire passage in the book of Numbers as alluding, prophetically, to Esther's future responsibility vis-à-vis Ahasuerus's genocidal decree. With as small a change as the removal of one dot in the word *ishah*, a secondary message suggests itself in the passage, a message that is the mirror image of the plain text:

> Any vow or restrictive oath that would cause excruciating hardship, the woman can affirm, or the woman can annul. [But] if she is silent, yes, silent, from day to day, then she will have affirmed all the vows or restrictions. She will have affirmed them, for she has been silent on the day she heard of them. And if she [tries to] annul after she [first] heard of it [and was silent], she bears his sin. These are the laws … of a [*na'ara*] in her father's house.

The word thus means "a [woman's] husband." (*ish* means "man," and the dot in the *heh* makes the word possessive, so that it means "her *ish*."). But Mordecai seems to be suggesting that the entire passage has a double meaning that comes alive if one makes the smallest of all conceivable adjustments, removing the dot from the *heh* at the end of that word. Stripped of its dot, the word *isha* means "woman" (the *heh* at the end of the word now indicates the feminine form of *ish*, rather than the possessive form). Once you read the word that way, the passage stands on its head. It alludes not to a man's power to annul the declaration of his wife, but a woman's power to annul the declaration of her husband. It refers to the precise situation Esther finds herself in.

The king has made a verbal declaration that will cause terrible pain. But the ink is not yet dry on the decree. Its efficacy is not a foregone conclusion. Esther can protest it – and in protesting it, Mordecai tells her, she can annul it.[3] According to Mordecai, Esther must act, not for the Jews' sake, but for her own. *Im hacharesh tacharishi*, if Esther makes herself deaf (Est. 4:14), if Esther tries to sit this crisis out in silence, to make herself deaf to what the king has said, she will thereby tacitly affirm the king's edict. And if that happens, she will bear responsibility, for as Rashi says, the person who stands silently by is responsible for the tragedy that results from the declaration they could have annulled. Yes, the Jews will be fine, one way or the other – God will see to it that salvation arises from elsewhere – but the choice that confronts Esther is what her own destiny will be. Will she speak out and go down in history as the one who tried to annul the evil decree? Or will she, through silence, become a de facto partner in upholding that very decree? If she chooses silence – her legacy will be destroyed along with Haman:

> You and your father's house will be destroyed. (Est. 4:14)

3. I do not mean to imply a legal, or halachic, equivalence between Esther and the *na'ara* described in the book of Numbers, or, for that matter, between Esther and that *na'ara*'s husband. According to Numbers, the prerogative to annul vows is the husband's. Moreover, in issuing an edict to destroy the Jews, the king has not, in the strict sense of the word, taken a vow. Hence, in a legal sense, the passage in Numbers does not apply to Esther's case. Nevertheless, by overtly interpolating language from the book of Numbers into Mordecai's speech to Esther, the Megilla seems to be suggesting a conceptual, if not a legal, equivalence between the situations. Esther, like the husband in the book of Numbers, has both the power and the responsibility to respond to an impetuous declaration made by a spouse. Like him, she can protest and annul the declaration of a spouse – or, by her silence, become a partner in delivering that declaration from the realm of potentiality into reality. If she remains silent, she, like the husband in Numbers, will bear responsibility for that declaration, whether she likes it or not.

FROM LOTS TO ANNULMENT

We are now in a position to understand the mysterious name of the holiday. As we noted earlier, the Megilla seems to be hinting that Purim is named for something Esther did, not just for something Haman did. But what does the name Purim, "lots," have to do with what Esther did?

Nothing – if you translate *pur* as "lots." But there's another translation available for *that* word as well, a translation borrowed from our passage in the book of Numbers:

> *Isha yekimenu; isha yeferenu.*
> The woman can affirm it; the woman can annul it.

As it turns out, the word Numbers uses for "annulling" the declaration of one's spouse, *yeferenu,* just happens to derive from the word *pur* – that is, from the three-letter root P-U-R. *Pur,* which in Ancient Persian or Aramaic means "lots," just happens, in Biblical Hebrew, to mean "annul."[4] In the context of the Megilla, then, the term *pur* refers not just to Haman's lots, but to the act that Mordecai told Esther she had the power to perform in the face of the king's decree: she could *annul* it.

We now understand the double meaning in the Megilla's explanation for why the holiday is called Purim. On one plane of meaning, it is called Purim because of Haman's *pur,* his lots. But on another, it is called that because of Esther's *pur,* her annulment of Haman's decree. If we look at the passage this way, here's how we'd read it: Haman tried to kill us, and to that end, he cast lots – the *pur*. But, the Megilla suggests, that's not the whole story concerning how the holiday came to bear this name. Esther, with

4. According to *Sefer HaShorashim,* the medieval dictionary of roots by Rabbi David Kimchi, the root of the Biblical Hebrew word "annul," as found in the book of Numbers, is P-U-R – the very letters that spell *pur*.

her back to the wall, managed to annul Haman's plotted genocide. And so, the Megilla concludes, that's why they called these days "Purim" – because of the *pur* (*hafur*).

In other words, the Megilla's explanation for the name Purim is deliciously ironic: in the end, they called these days Purim not for Haman's "lots," but for Esther's "annulments." Haman had wanted the day to be known for his *pur*, his instrument of chance. Instead, the fate of the Jews was determined by another *pur*, by Esther's act of *hafara*. And that's why they called the day Purim: because of her *pur*, not his.

Isha yeferenu.
A woman will annul it.

Esther, faced with an apparent fait accompli, did not stand by silently. She did not give her tacit assent to a decree she could hardly hope to change. Instead, she found a way to annul it. And *that's* why they called the day Purim.[5]

5. Interestingly, the *Zohar*, Judaism's prime mystical text, sees Purim as related thematically to another holiday bearing a phonetically similar name: the Day of Atonement, known in Hebrew as *Yom Kippurim* (since the *kaf* prefix in Hebrew can mean "like," *Yom Kippurim* can be read as "a day that is like Purim"). In light of our analysis of Purim's double meaning – "lots" and "vows" – the *Zohar*'s linkage seems to take on a dramatic quality – for fascinatingly, each of these two meanings of the word *pur* finds expression in the two holidays. Purim is a day Haman selected by lots, but lots are associated with Yom Kippur as well: a lottery is held on Yom Kippur to decide the fate of two identical goats in the Temple service of the day (see Lev. 16:8). Similarly, Purim, as we've seen, borrows its name and motif from the annulment of vows described in the book of Numbers, and by long-standing custom, the Yom Kippur prayers begin with the *Kol Nidrei* service, dedicated to, of all things, the annulment of unfulfilled vows the congregation might have undertaken during the previous year (see, at length, *Tikkunei Zohar*, introduction, 57b).

PAIRS OF SEVENS IN ESTHER'S NINTH

> *Isha yekimenu; isha yeferenu.*
> A woman can affirm; a woman can annul.

In the final analysis, this one phrase from the book of Numbers ends up being the crux of the entire Megilla. In four words, it pithily summarizes the strategy that ultimately granted Esther victory in her efforts to save the Jews. Moreover, as if to demonstrate its centrality in the Megilla's closing act, there are no less than fourteen allusions to this phrase throughout the book of Esther's ninth, and penultimate, chapter.

To find the fourteen allusions, focus on the roots of the verbs in the phrase from Numbers. The root for "affirm" is K-Y-M. If you scan the ninth chapter of Esther, you will find this root everywhere. Just about everything that happens in the chapter is an act of K-Y-M, affirmation. Mordecai instructs the Jews to *affirm* Purim as a holiday. The Jews then do it, and they *affirm* the day they celebrated spontaneously as a yearly, official holiday. Afterward, Esther gives the royal imprimatur to the day, *affirming* Mordecai's decree that the day be celebrated. All these verbs are variations on the verb K-Y-M, a verb borrowed from our favorite passage in the book of Numbers. If you count up the occurrences of K-Y-M in the ninth chapter of the Megilla, you will find no less than seven of them.

But K-Y-M is not the only verb borrowed from Numbers that appears seven times in the ninth chapter of Esther. The verse in Numbers continues:

> *Isha yekimenu; isha yeferenu.*

The woman can annul, too. As we've mentioned, the root for "annul" is *pur*, and seven times, we meet with variations of *pur* in the Megilla's ninth chapter. Usually, it means "lots," or the name of the holiday, "Purim." But, as we've suggested, it sometimes seems to mean "annulment" as well.[6] The story of Esther's triumph is really the story of these two roots, K-Y-M and P-U-R, fused together. To put it concisely, if somewhat cryptically: Neither one alone would grant victory; in the end, she had to use both. She needed both to "affirm" and to "annul." To explain: At first, Esther tried just to *annul* the decree against the Jews. That is, she tried to oppose and thereby nullify the king's written decree. But whenever she tried to do this, she failed.

The first time she tried this was when she attempted, in a somewhat backhanded fashion, to get the king to annul the decree. She asked him to save her life by annulling Haman's decree, but the king didn't do it. Instead, he saved her and killed Haman – but left in place Haman's edict threatening the rest of the Jews.

Later, Esther tried again. This time, she made her plea directly, asking the king to repeal the writ threatening her people. In so doing, she risked her life by boldly declaring her loyalty to her countrymen. Yet she again failed. The king denied her request, insisting on the sanctity of Persian law. In Persia, the king declared, written decrees could never be revoked. It seemed that all was lost.

Esther tried one last time, though – and this time, she succeeded. What, in the end, did she do differently this last time? The last time, she both "affirmed" and "annulled." Rather than futilely pleading with the king to annul a written decree he didn't want to annul, she did the opposite, leaving that decree in place and concentrating instead on *affirming* a second, contradictory royal decree. Remember, the king had allowed Esther and Mordecai to

6. Indeed, the seventh and last occurrence of the root P-U-R (annul/lots) in the ninth chapter of Esther actually coincides with the seventh and last occurrence of the root K-Y-M (affirm). The seventh occurrence of each root just happens to occur side by side in the very same verse:

Uma'amar Esther kiyam divrei hapurim ha'eleh.

And the decree of Esther affirmed these words of Purim. (Est. 9:32) write what they pleased concerning the Jews. By itself, that didn't amount to much. What good is writing anything when the authorization for a pogrom to destroy you is set in stone? But Mordecai and Esther weren't daunted. With the king's license, they issued a second decree in his name, giving the Jews the right to go on the offensive. Then they focused their efforts on *affirming* that decree to every extent possible. They built it up more and more, creating out of thin air an impression that the palace actually cared about the welfare of the Jews and would back them in the conflict against their enemies.

To sum up: Esther initially focused all her energy on annulling the first decree, but the more she pressed, the less successful she was. In the end, she was able to achieve victory only by both "affirming" and "annulling" – or, more precisely, by "affirming" the second decree as a way of "annulling" the first one. In the prophetic words of the book of Numbers:

> *Isha yekimenu ve'isha yeferenu.*
> A woman will affirm it; a woman will annul it.

Part III

Déjà Vu All Over Again

Preface to Part III

The Mordecai Verses

We have one last mystery to unravel. We talked about three verses traditionally read aloud by the entire congregation during the chanting of the Megilla on Purim. These verses, as you'll recall, disproportionately focus on Mordecai, and we wanted to understand why, of all the verses in the Megilla, our tradition has singled out these for special emphasis.[1]

To recap the problem: one of these verses details the obscure lineage of Mordecai (he is the son of Shimi, the son of Kish, etc.), a point that seems to have no bearing on anything else in the Megilla.

---

1. One of these verses talks about Mordecai's parade. It recounts how Mordecai appeared in Shushan with a big gold crown on his head, and how the city of Shushan erupted in joy. Based on our preceding analysis of the Megilla, we can now see why this event was so pivotal, and why it is worthy of special mention: Mordecai's parade was a remarkable and daring bluff that helped turn the tide of public opinion, creating the impression that the palace backed the Jewish cause far more than it did. So giving special attention to this verse is certainly understandable. Nevertheless, the special prominence given to the other two "Mordecai verses" seems odd, as we shall explain momentarily.

Another (the very last verse of the Megilla, actually) emphasizes that "Mordecai the Jew was second in charge to King Ahasuerus; he was great among the Jews, and pleasing to most of his brethren." But why is it so crucial for us to remember that Mordecai got to act as second in charge to the king?[2] Why is this the most fitting way to end the Megilla? Moreover, what's this about Mordecai being pleasing to most of his brethren? Why do we need to be reminded that his poll numbers were pretty high, that most, but not all, of the populace sort of liked him? Why not just end the Megilla with "and they all lived happily ever after"?

As we'll see in the pages that follow, these questions are a window onto yet another unexpected face of the Megilla, one which grounds the Purim story more deeply in its historical context. In the preceding pages, we have laid the necessary groundwork for examining this story, as we've worked to reconstruct the hidden narrative in the last three chapters of the Megilla. Let us try, then, to build on this foundation and see what discoveries might still await us.

2. It could just be that the verses are special because of their placement. The first verse introduces us to Mordecai for the very first time, and the other is the last in the Megilla. But this doesn't really eliminate the questions we've posed; it just prompts us to reformulate them. Why does the verse that introduces Mordecai give us such a long winded rundown of his genealogy? And why is it appropriate that the Megilla closes with a verse that revels in Mordecai's great, but not universal, popularity?

Chapter Eleven

A Telltale Phrase

In reading the Megilla, it can seem as if the Purim narrative could have begun with "Once upon a time in Ancient Persia" and ended with "happily ever after," and you wouldn't need to know anything more about Jewish history to understand it. In fact, though, the Purim story is part of a larger tale. A great deal of the Megilla's meaning lies in how its narrative interacts with the larger kaleidoscope of Jewish history.

REVISITING ESTHER'S MOST DESPERATE HOUR

To see this larger message of the Book of Esther, we need to reinsert ourselves into the drama of the Megilla's final chapters. We need to go back and take another look at the crossroads in the Megilla that was Esther's most desperate hour.

When was that moment? As we argued earlier, it wasn't when Esther first approached the king to ask that he attend her party. Nor was it when she rose from the banquet to reveal Haman as the man who threatened her life. It was much later, when all seemed deceptively calm and sunny. Haman had been hanged, Esther and Mordecai had been suitably rewarded, but Haman's malice lingered. His planned pogrom was still slated to strike. It was then that Esther approached the king and asked him, begged him, to annul Haman's decree.

When she took that action, we argued, she risked her own life more daringly than ever before. Until that point, Esther could hide; she had tried to distract the king with suspicions of a love triangle, with the thought that Haman might take her away from him. Now, though, with Haman dead, she has lost her foil. Now, her only chance of saving the Jews is to lay bare her true loyalties and hope that the king will spare her people as a personal favor to his queen.

When Esther chooses to do just that, she places herself in a dangerous position indeed. She had ascended the throne as a stateless girl who would become the king's new "Mother Persia." Now, her newly declared loyalty to the Jewish people could threaten all that. Would the king see her as a traitor, as a pretender?

Esther makes her appeal. But as if to confirm that she's on thin ice, the king – for the first time in the entire story – does not give her what she wants. He reacts with annoyance. There are no niceties anymore, no more talk of giving her "half the kingdom" if only she asks for it. He lists all the favors he has already done for the Jews and refuses to revoke the decree, arguing that it is set in stone. Esther and Mordecai are left to parlay what the king *does* give them – an apparently useless license to write what they want concerning the doomed Jews – into a plan that might, just might, save her countrymen, despite the king's utter lack of interest in helping their cause.

Right there, as Esther finally risks all by revealing her deepest loyalties – right there, if we listen closely to her words, we will notice something strange: we've heard them before.

A BORROWED POIGNANCY

Esther said to the king:

> If I am pleasing to you, let the king write to repeal [Haman's] decrees…for how could I possibly [stand by and] watch the terrible [fate] that befalls my people; how could I possibly [stand by and] watch the destruction of my own kin? (Est. 8:5–6)

"How could I stand by and watch the terrible [fate] that befalls my people?" asks the queen. Her words are laden with poignancy, but it is a poignancy borrowed from another famous biblical figure, who said precisely the same thing somewhere earlier in the Hebrew Bible. With the exception of a single syllable, Esther's words are a direct quote from a declaration made centuries before her birth.

The source for her words can be found in the book of Genesis, toward the end of the Joseph saga. In that extended story, Benjamin, one of the children of Jacob, faced the possibility of imprisonment at the hands of an Egyptian official. Benjamin's brother Judah pleaded with that official for Benjamin's safe return, saying that he could not bear to return home to his father without Benjamin, his father's beloved son. His words, "How could I bear to see the terrible [fate] that befalls my father [when he realizes Benjamin is gone]?" (Gen. 44:34), are the words that Esther echoes so many years later, when she asks Ahasuerus rhetorically, "How could I bear to see the terrible [fate] that befalls my people?"

In all the Hebrew Bible, this particular phrase – in Hebrew, *bera asher yimtza et* – appears only twice. The first time is at the beginning of the Bible, in Genesis, when Judah uses it. The second and last time is at the close of the biblical era, when Esther uses it.[1] Now what are we to make of this? It may be that Esther uses the phrase simply because it sounds nice. It sounded nice when Judah said it; it sounds nice when she says it. What's wrong with drawing a little inspiration from those who came before you? But there may be something else going on here.

It may be that Esther quotes from Judah not because she was leafing through the biblical equivalent of *Bartlett's Familiar Quotations* for any old phrase that sounded poignant, but because Judah's situation was *uniquely* meaningful to her. That is, there was something special about her circumstance that resonated, very particularly, with the one Judah found himself in long ago. Was something happening *now,* at this particular juncture, that could only be understood with reference to what had happened *then*?

WHEN LIGHTNING STRIKES TWICE

The suspicion that something unique connects these two moments in history deepens when we realize that this is not the only time Queen Esther alludes to the drama involving Judah, Benjamin, and Jacob; Esther borrows a phrase from that same story in Genesis on another occasion.

When Mordecai first approached Esther and urged her to go to the king, you will recall that Esther initially demurred, protesting that it was too dangerous, but Mordecai insisted that she go. Now pay attention to the exact words Esther uses when she resigns herself to enter Ahasuerus's chambers. She says:

---

1. In Hebrew, Esther's words are nearly identical to Judah's, but she finishes off Judah's phrase differently: Judah spoke about the evil that would befall "my father," whereas Esther speaks of the evil that would befall "my people." Nevertheless, even here, the similarity is striking, for in Hebrew, the words "my father" and "my people" are phonetically similar. Here are the phrases in Hebrew, transliterated:

   Esther: *Bera asher yimtza et ami*
   Judah: *Bera asher yimtza et avi*

> I will go to the king against the rules, and…
> *ka'asher avadeti, avadeti*
> If I am lost, then so be it; I am lost. (Est. 4:16)

Where else in the Bible do we have a phrase like that, a phrase with similar literary structure and similar meaning? A phrase that opens with the word *ka'asher* ("if" or "when") and is immediately followed by a doubled verb (e.g., *avadeti, avadeti*)? A phrase that indicates the speaker's resignation to the possibility of failure, as this phrase does? There is only one other time in the entire Bible that we find a phrase with all these elements, and it's in the same story as before, the story involving Judah, Jacob, and Benjamin. Jacob is reluctant to allow Benjamin to travel from Canaan to Egypt, fearing that something might happen to him along the way. And when Jacob finally decides to allow Benjamin – his precious, youngest child – to go, he reconciles himself to the fear of losing him by saying:

> *Veka'asher shakolti, shakolti*
> And if I am to lose [Benjamin], then so be it; I shall lose [him]. (Gen. 43:14)

When Esther speaks of her own possible demise in going before the king, she echoes Jacob's words. When Esther says, *Veka'asher avadeti, avadeti* (If I am lost, then so be it; I shall be lost), it is the only other time in the Bible such a formulation is ever used.[2]

---

2. The verb Jacob uses twice, *shakolti*, literally means "to become bereft," to lose a child. Jacob's phrase begins with the Hebrew word *ka'asher* and is followed by a doubled verb: *shakolti, shakolti*, each in the first person, past tense. The only other time in the entire Bible *ka'asher* appears along with a similarly conjugated doubled verb is when Esther says *ka'asher avadeti, avadeti*.

DECIPHERING PARALLEL TEXTS

So that makes two times Esther quotes language from the story involving Judah, Jacob, and Benjamin. Had it happened once, maybe you'd chalk it up to happenstance; you could say the author of the Megilla found a nice turn of phrase somewhere and echoed it, without the context mattering all that much. But twice? That doesn't seem like happenstance.

It's hard to resist the suspicion that there's something about that earlier story of Judah, Jacob, and Benjamin that uniquely connects it to Esther's saga. The author of the Megilla seems to have an agenda here, a reason for consistently reminding us of the same trio of protagonists in the book of Genesis.[3] It's almost as if the writer of the Megilla is winking knowingly at us. But what does the wink mean?

When in one story, the Bible repeatedly quotes from an earlier biblical narrative, the text is conveying something profound to the careful reader. Through these linkages, the Bible is creating its own internal commentary on the meaning of its text. It is saying: *If you really want to understand what's going on over here, you need first to understand what's going on over there.* You need to see the second story in light of the first. The Bible, by playing connect the dots with us, is speaking to us, helping us discern layers of meaning beneath its surface – if only we bother to listen to what it has to say.

What do we need to do to "listen"? For starters, we need to look more carefully at the verses from Genesis that the Megilla is paraphrasing. We need to perceive their role within the larger

3. As we shall see in the forthcoming sequel to this book, these two examples of phraseology in Esther that hark back to the Joseph story are actually just the tip of the iceberg. The literary links between Esther and the Joseph saga are breathtakingly extensive. We shall consider the broad meaning of these links in that forthcoming sequel. For now, we will confine our focus to the particular ties between Esther's words and the story of Judah, Jacob, and the plight of Benjamin.

Joseph saga. Then we will be able to return to the Purim story and understand why the Megilla quotes them.

Let's go back, then, and briefly review the Joseph story, paying special attention to the interactions involving Judah, Jacob, and Benjamin. Then we will be able to perceive the astonishing window these verses open onto the meaning of Esther's actions.

Chapter Twelve

The Hardest Words to Say

A HOUSE DIVIDED

How did Benjamin get to be the center of attention at the dénouement of the Joseph story? To understand this – and the full import of the interaction between Judah, Benjamin, and Jacob – we need to review briefly some familiar stories in the book of Genesis that predate the conflict between Joseph and his brothers.

Genesis records that Jacob, in his youth, impersonated his brother, Esau, and thereby took through deception the blessings their father, Isaac, meant to bestow upon Esau. In the wake of that act, Jacob ran away from Canaan to escape his brother's wrath. He went to Haran, where his mother's family came from, and sought out his uncle Laban. In so doing, he encountered Laban's daughter Rachel by a well. Captivated by her, Jacob asked Laban for Rachel's hand in marriage. Laban consented – on condition that Jacob work for him for seven years.

The seven years pass, and the long-anticipated wedding takes place. The next morning, however, Jacob wakes up to the realization that Laban has deceived him. The woman behind the veil was Leah, Rachel's older sister, not Rachel herself. Jacob confronts Laban, demanding to know why he tricked him. To this, Laban replies simply:

> We don't do it that way, in our place, to give the younger before the firstborn. (Gen. 29:26)

Laban's response is a not-so-subtle dig at Jacob. Jacob had, of course, put "the younger before the firstborn" back in Canaan when he, the younger brother, dressed up as Esau, the older, and took the blessing of the firstborn meant for Esau. "We don't do it that way in *our* place," Laban tells him. Over here, we do things right; we put the older first. Laban's flippant defense of his treachery seems calculated to give Jacob the message that what goes around, comes around. Jacob had deceived his father by dressing up one child as another; now, he himself has fallen victim to trickery in a very similar game of dress-up. In the end, Laban tells Jacob that he will give him Rachel's hand in marriage after all – but only in return for another seven years of work. Jacob agrees, and in short order, finds himself married to both sisters. A rivalry for Jacob's love is born between the sisters, a rivalry tragically expressed in the names of their children:

> And Leah conceived and bore a child, and she named him Reuben – for she said: "God has seen [*ru'a*] my suffering [*be'oni*], and now, my husband will love me." (Gen. 29:32)

> And she conceived again and bore a child and said: "God has heard [*shama*] that I am unloved" – and she named him Simeon. (Gen. 29:33)

Child after child is born to Leah, until Rachel finally bears a child too. She names him Joseph, declaring that God has "gathered in" (*asaf*) her sense of shame at her childlessness (Gen. 30:23, with Rashi). Rachel then gives birth to one last child – and dies in the process. That last child is Benjamin.

Ironically, the name the dying Rachel gives this very last child of Jacob is almost a phonetic replica of the phrase Leah used when she gave birth to Jacob's first child, Reuben. Leah had said: *Ra'a Hashem be'oni,* "God has seen my suffering," while Rachel calls Benjamin *ben oni,* "the child of my suffering" (see Gen. 35:18 with Rashi).

The names of the children, so bound up in the pain of their respective mothers, seem to presage the fact that the sisters' rivalry for Jacob's love will filter down to their children's generation as well. And indeed, we come to learn that Jacob loved Joseph, Rachel's firstborn, more than all his other children – and he made a special coat for him to signify that special bond. Joseph's brothers perceive that Jacob loves Joseph more than he loves them, and tensions between the sets of brothers begin to build. Eventually, these tensions explode in what has come to be known as the sale of Joseph.

One day, Joseph's brothers see him coming to greet them, and they plot to do away with him. They strip Joseph of his coat and cast him into a pit. They do not leave him there to perish, however. Instead, they follow the advice of Judah, fourth son of Leah, who counsels that they should instead sell Joseph to merchants heading to Egypt. Joseph travels to Egypt and begins life there as a slave.

JOSEPH AND THE BROTHERS MEET AGAIN

Years later, Joseph and his brothers meet again, but by then, circumstances have changed. Joseph, who successfully interpreted a dream of Pharaoh's that forecast seven years of famine, has risen to become second in charge to the king. When the promised famine arrives, Jacob's family members find themselves short on food in Canaan, and Jacob dispatches them to Egypt for grain. Or, to be precise, he dispatches *most* of them to Egypt. He keeps Benjamin with him in Canaan, making certain that the last remaining son of Rachel stays safe at home.

When the brothers arrive in Egypt seeking food for their families, they encounter the high Egyptian official who controls the disbursement of grain. Little do they know that this official happens to be their long-lost brother, Joseph. Joseph recognizes them, but they do not recognize him. The stage is now set for a drama that will place Benjamin at the center of a storm.

Joseph speaks harshly to the brothers. He accuses them of being spies and tells them that he will grant them no further audience until they bring their last remaining brother back to Egypt with them, the brother they say they've left at home. When the brothers arrive back in Canaan and tell Jacob the news, he is despondent and refuses to allow Benjamin to go. Rachel herself had died. Since then, Jacob had also lost her eldest son, Joseph; Benjamin is now all that is left of her. Jacob will not take the chance of losing the last surviving remnant of the beloved girl he met at the well.

With their supplies dwindling, Reuben makes an attempt to get their father to reconsider. Jacob rebuffs him; Benjamin will remain safe by his side, no matter what. Finally, Judah speaks:

> Send the lad with me, and let us get up and go; let us live and not die.... I will personally guarantee his safety. If I don't bring him back to you and stand him up here before you, I will have sinned against you all the days of my life. (Gen. 43:8–9)

Jacob gives in to Judah and entrusts Benjamin to his care. And it is then that Jacob utters the first phrase that echoes in the book of Esther:

> Let God grant mercy to you in the eyes of [the Egyptian].... And as for me, if I am to lose [Benjamin), then so be it; I shall lose him. (Gen. 43:14)

BENJAMIN, SEIZED

Judah has promised to deliver Benjamin back and forth safely, but little does he know how heavily the deck will be stacked against Benjamin's safe return. For when the brothers arrive back in Egypt along with Benjamin, Joseph – in their eyes, simply "the Egyptian" – has arranged a surprise for them.

Joseph instructs his men, who are packing the brothers' bags full of food and supplies, to secretly place his own royal goblet in Benjamin's sack. As the brothers depart the city, Joseph dispatches his troops to overtake them, and when they do, they speak of recovering a stolen goblet. Judah protests, telling them that he and his brothers are innocent; the last thing they would do is steal from the Egyptian who has so magnanimously provided them with food. Judah, in his zeal, actually offers to kill anyone found to have stolen the goblet.

He further promises that he and the rest of the brothers will allow themselves to remain in Egypt as prisoners and slaves if any of the brothers are found guilty.

Joseph's men search the brothers' sacks. And, of course, the goblet is found in Benjamin's luggage. The brothers are stunned. Joseph kindly declines Judah's offer to kill the thief and imprison them all, and instead tells them they are all free to go home – except for the thief himself. Benjamin must stay in Egypt with him, as his personal slave.

THE PROMISE KEEPER

If you were Judah, you could certainly be excused if you gave up at this point and headed home. Yes, Jacob might incessantly mourn Benjamin's loss, but the reality is that Jacob and everyone else should count themselves lucky that Benjamin, caught red-handed, was still alive at all. The logical course of action, the prudent choice, would be to cut your losses and leave – while you still can.

But Judah does not embrace the prudent choice. He does not leave. He stays right there and addresses the Egyptian official with a risky but heartfelt plea. He tells the Egyptian official how reluctant his father had been to send his beloved son Benjamin, last remaining child of his precious Rachel, to Egypt:

> My father said to us [at that time]: "You know that my wife gave birth to [only] two [children]. One left me and was apparently torn apart by wild beasts; I've never seen him since. And now you will take this one, too, from me; and [what if] a terrible accident happens to him? You will send me down to my grave in despair." (Gen. 44:27–29)

Judah continues, telling the official what he fears will happen should Benjamin fail to return:

> And now, if I come back to my father and the lad is not with me – well, my father's soul is bound up in his soul. When he sees that the lad is not here, he'll die. (Gen. 44:30–31)

Judah explains that he has personally guaranteed Benjamin's safety to his father, and beseeches the official to allow him, Judah, to take Benjamin's place as his servant, so that Benjamin might return to his father. And then we hear those words that resonate, once again, in the book of Esther:

> For how can I go back to my father without the child by my side, lest I see the terrible [fate] that will befall my father. (Gen. 44:34)

Imagine how difficult it must have been for Judah, a child of Leah, to say these words, to recognize in so direct a fashion how much his father loved Benjamin, the child of his mother's rival, and be willing to sacrifice everything to honor that love. "You know that my wife [i.e., Rachel] gave birth to [only] two [children]," Judah had said earlier, paraphrasing his father Jacob (Gen. 44:27). "My wife" – as if he had only one. What about Leah? Did she even exist in Jacob's mind? And Judah continues, telling the Egyptian: "[My father's] soul is bound up with [Benjamin's] soul." Judah knows that his father and Benjamin share a special bond, that his father would want Benjamin by his side more than he would want Judah there. He looks these facts in the eye and is willing to accept them. More than that, he is willing to sacrifice everything for them.[1]

The Egyptian official listening to Judah's speech is uniquely suited to understand all these implications of Judah's words. After all, that official is none other than Joseph, who is overcome by what he hears. He can no longer hold back his emotions, and he reveals his true identity to his shocked brothers. The brothers return to Canaan with the news that Joseph is still alive, and Jacob travels to Egypt for a tearful reunion with the son he had never dreamed to see again.

---

1. Jacob's intense identification with Benjamin comes through in other ways, too, sometimes more subtly. Judah, for example, explains to the Egyptian that, after Rachel's first child had been lost, Benjamin alone was all that remained to Jacob from his mother (Gen. 44:20). The Hebrew for "he alone remained" is *vayivater hu levado*. Hebrew readers of the Bible will recognize that phrase, which appears only one other time in the Torah – notably, as a description of Jacob himself. Just before Jacob confronts the angel with whom he wrestles, the text says *vayivater Ya'akov levado* – Jacob remained alone, all by himself on one side of the river, having placed his family safely on the other side (Gen. 32:25). By describing Benjamin in precisely the same terms as had applied to his father, Judah seems to suggest that Benjamin "is" Jacob, personifies him, somehow, in the next generation. Jacob lives on through Benjamin; he is his legacy – at least in Jacob's own eyes.

BACK TO THE FUTURE

In the book of Esther, at the very end of the Bible, we hear once more those seven climactic words with which Judah closed his speech. They echo in Esther's plea to Ahasuerus, at the moment she risked her life most audaciously.

Let's now try to understand why.

Chapter Thirteen

Private Benjamin

ESCAPING ANACHRONISM

What group of people is the Purim story about? In other words, who were the people Haman plotted to kill? Who were the people that Mordecai and Esther managed to save?

The question seems too obvious even to warrant an answer. We all know who these people were. They were the Jews. Purim, after all, is a Jewish holiday. Who else would we expect the holiday to be about?

But let's say I pressed you a bit. Sure, the Megilla is about the Jews. But what exactly do you mean by "the Jews"?

At this point, you might become a bit exasperated: *Who were the Jews? You know, the Israelites, the House of Jacob – pick your label; the people who count Abraham as their father, who believe in monotheism; the ones who eat lox and bagels and brought good dill pickles into the world. Those guys.*

As if to reiterate the obvious, you might open a Megilla and point to the many times the book speaks of the *Yehudim*. Haman plotted to kill the *Yehudim*. Esther asked the *Yehudim* to fast on her behalf. The *Yehudim* celebrated when they were saved. Everyone knows that *Yehudim* is the Hebrew word for "Jews." If you have any doubt, just go to Israel, where they speak Hebrew, and see how people use the word.

All the Jews there call themselves *Yehudim*. Israel calls itself a *medina Yehudit,* a Jewish state. So if there were any question, that about settles it, right? Case closed. But *is* the case closed? What we really need to know is not what the term *Yehudim* means now, but what it meant back then, when the Bible was written. Has the word evolved, and if so, can we discern the word's original meaning?

Well, if in biblical times the word *Yehudim* really meant "Jews," the word should appear just about everywhere in the Five Books of Moses. After all, the Pentateuch is mostly about Jews. So whenever the Torah refers to the people as a whole, it should call them *Yehudim*. But it doesn't; the Torah calls the Jews the children of Israel. It calls them the House of Jacob. But before the final days of the Second Commonwealth, at the close of biblical history, it never actually calls them *Yehudim*.[1] The word *Yehudim,* when it appeared in the Megilla, was of very recent vintage – no more than a few generations old.

Why all of a sudden, at the close of biblical history, around the time of the Megilla, does the Bible feel compelled to refer to these Israelites in a whole new way? Who, exactly, *were* these *Yehudim*? To find the answer, we need to consider the particular circumstances in which the Megilla was written. Let's step back and recall what was happening among the Jews at that juncture in history.

---

1. The word appears a couple of times in II Kings (e.g., 16:6 and 25:25) and the book of Jeremiah (e.g., 32:12 and elsewhere), but never before this.

THE MEGILLA'S HISTORICAL CONTEXT

Ever since the reign of Solomon, son of David, the Jewish people was split into two distinct groupings: there was the Northern Kingdom, controlled (at least initially) by the tribe of Ephraim, and consisting of most of the twelve tribes of ancient Israel, and there was the Southern Kingdom, controlled by the tribe of Judah, but also including the much smaller and weaker tribe of Benjamin, which was Judah's neighbor geographically. The Northern Kingdom was often called the Kingdom of Israel, or "Ephraim" for short; the Southern Kingdom was usually known as the Kingdom of Judah.

For many years, these kingdoms lived side by side. Then, in the seventh century BCE, the Assyrian king Tiglath-Pileser, followed by his successor, Sennacherib, invaded from the north. The Kingdom of Judah suffered losses but ultimately staved off Sennacherib; the Northern Kingdom was not as fortunate. Sennacherib defeated Ephraim, took possession of the north, and exiled the ten tribes, scattering them throughout his empire. They have not been heard from since.

All that remained of sovereign Israel was now the Southern Kingdom, the Kingdom of Judah. For several generations, Judah held on, but eventually, this kingdom, too, fell to invaders. Eventually, the Babylonian king Nebuchadnezzar invaded Judah, conquered Jerusalem, and burned the Temple. He, too, exiled his vanquished enemy, but unlike Sennacherib, he did not scatter them. The exiled Judahites managed, more or less, to remain together in the land of their captors, and they set up intact communities in Babylon.

One of the things that sustained them was hope. While the Temple still stood, the prophet Jeremiah had foretold that exile would come, but he had also prophesied that the exile would be short-lived. In a span of seventy years, Jeremiah said, God would redeem Judah, and the exiled people would be free to return to the Promised Land.

During those seventy years, a new power rose to prominence on the world scene. Cyrus the Great defeated Babylonia and established Persia and Media as the greatest, most far-flung empire the ancient world had ever seen. As part of his conquest, Cyrus took possession of the territory of ancient Israel, and became the ruler of the beleaguered, exiled Judahites.

All this set the stage for the drama of the Megilla. Shortly after the reign of Cyrus, Ahasuerus (identified by some as Xerxes I) ascended the throne of the new empire, and the events we know as the story of Purim unfolded.

A KINGDOM'S REMNANTS

So now it's time to get back to our question: Who are the Megilla's *Yehudim*? The answer now seems fairly obvious. *Yehudim* is nothing but the plural of Yehuda – or, in English, the name "Judah." In the context of the period, then, the word *Yehudim* would have meant "Judahites," people from the Kingdom of Yehuda, exiled remnants of the Judahite nation.

Over time, the term *Yehudim* took on other connotations. As memories of autonomous life under the kings of Judah faded, the term *Yehudim* gradually lost its particular tribal, or national, connotation. Eventually, *Yehudim* came to signify "Jews," those who adhere to the faith of Judaism, more than it signified those who belong to the nation of Judah. But it wasn't always that way. In the days of Purim, it certainly wasn't that way. The newly exiled remnants of the Judahite kingdom thought of themselves as *Yehudim*, Judahites. And that's how the Persians would have thought of them, too.

Of course, like any label, the term *Yehudim* was an oversimplification. Even when the Southern Kingdom was alive and well, it was never the case that every citizen of that kingdom was a member of the tribe of Judah; that is, not all *Yehudim* were blood descendants of Judah, son of Jacob. First of all, there were more or less open borders between the two kingdoms of Israel, and there was always merchant traffic between them, so some members of the ten tribes would have resided in the Kingdom of Judah. Moreover, as foreign invasion hit Ephraim, the ranks of Judah would have swelled with refugees from the North, from the ten tribes. But even more significantly, as mentioned above, the Kingdom of Judah also included the territory – and the population – of a distinctly separate group: the tribe of Benjamin.

The Megilla thus tells us that Haman threatened to destroy all the *Yehudim*. From Haman's perspective, these aliens might all have seemed the same; their internal differences were of no moment to him. But that's not to say that there weren't any differences among them; there were. Tribal affiliation still existed in Israel.

DIVIDED LOYALTIES

Let us listen carefully, then, to an often-overlooked verse in the Megilla that we wondered about before. Earlier in this book, we asked why the verse that introduces Mordecai to us is singled out for special treatment, why it is one of the four special verses read aloud by the congregation before being chanted by the Megilla's reader. If it's called the "Megilla of Esther," why don't we give Esther's introduction the same star-spangled treatment? The answer is now evident: Mordecai's introduction is important not just because it heralds the entrance of a hero; it is important because of what it tells us about this hero. Listen again, closely, to what this verse (Est. 2:5) is actually saying:

> There was a certain *Yehudi* in the capital city of Shushan, and his name was Mordecai, the son of Yair, the son of Shimi, the son of Kish.

And then the surprise twist:

He was a Benjamite man [*ish Yemini*].

The plot thickens. To the world at large, Mordecai is an *ish Yehudi*, a man from Judea, like any other. He was exiled from Jerusalem along with all the other Judahites during the days of Jeconiah, king of Judah (Est. 2:6). But in truth, he does not hail from the tribe of Judah at all. He is from the tribe of Benjamin. Yes, in a global sense, Mordecai is part of the Judahite nation; but he is still an *ish Yemini*; his primary family ties are to his Benjamite brethren.

The Megilla tells us that Mordecai and Esther come from the same family, so the same applies to her. She is a Judahite – but she is from the tribe of Benjamin. And these little facts about lineage make a big difference. For as Mordecai and Esther fight to save the embattled Jews, as long as the interests of the exiled Benjamites and the Judahites converge, all is well and good. But what will happen if and when the interests of the two groups don't converge?

Judah and Benjamin. It all comes down to Judah and Benjamin. We've heard all this before, haven't we?

RISKING ONE FOR MANY

Esther becomes queen, and one fine day, Mordecai sends word to her that Haman is plotting to kill the exiled remnants of the Southern Kingdom in a massive, worldwide pogrom. Esther at first does not wish to act. She protests that it is too dangerous. For a month now, she has not been called before the king, and if she invades his private chambers without invitation, he may well kill her on the spot. Mordecai tells her that this, regrettably, is a risk she must be prepared to take. He exhorts her not to keep silent in the face of this calamity, not to look after her own personal welfare by seeking the safety of the palace. Instead, she must risk her life, if necessary, to save the *Yehudim*.

Long ago, the welfare of the entire Jewish family was threatened, and the question of whether or not the family would survive came down to whether Benjamin's fate would be risked. Now, that family has become a people, and once again the question of whether it will survive has come down to whether "Benjamin" will be risked.

Back then, it was the decision of a father: in order to procure food for his starving family, he would have to allow his precious Benjamin to face a potentially malevolent foreign ruler. Would he risk Benjamin's life and allow him to go? Now, it is the decision of a Benjamite woman who has become queen. In order to avert the destruction of the people, she would have to face a potentially malevolent foreign ruler herself. Would she, the scion of Benjamin, risk her own life and go?

Jacob had at first said no, but then allowed himself to be convinced. Esther would first say no, but she too would allow herself to be convinced. Esther would finally agree to go to the king. And when she did, she would quote Jacob almost verbatim in openly accepting the possibility that "precious Benjamin" might not make it back alive:

> Jacob: *Ka'asher shakolti, shakolti*
> And if I am to lose [Benjamin], then so be it; I shall lose [him]. (Gen. 43:14)
>
> Esther: *Ka'asher avadeti, avadeti*
> If I am lost, then so be it; I shall be lost. (Est. 4:16)

Jacob had hoped that Benjamin's mere appearance before the Egyptian ruler would persuade him to provide the life-saving food his family needed. He hoped that a true showdown between Benjamin and that ruler would never be necessary. Likewise, Esther hoped that appearing before the king would be enough to save the threatened Jews, that a true showdown with the king would never be necessary. Unfortunately, they were both wrong.

ESTHER'S FINAL DILEMMA

Esther's hopes for a quick resolution are dashed. She tries valiantly to foil Haman's plot, but her gambit of stoking the king's suspicions about Haman falls short of its goal. The king kills Haman, but Haman's decrees remain on the books. Now Esther has no more tricks up her sleeve. All hopes of political artifice have slipped away. What will Esther do now?

It is now that the interests of Benjamin and Judah truly diverge. Esther and Mordecai have won the favor of the king; he will likely grant them license to shelter those close to them from the killing that is to come. She will be able to gather a finite number of people, as many as possible from her extended Benjamite family, into the palace and shield them from the gathering storm. But the rest of the Judahites? The tens of thousands from the tribe of Judah? What, really, could she be expected to do for them?

If Esther had any pangs of guilt at the unfortunate demise of the Judahites, she could soothe her conscience with the pleasant knowledge that she had tried, she really had, to do what she could to save them. She had tried and failed. Her attempt to create the suspicion of a love triangle was daring, brilliant – but it didn't quite work. Esther could well argue to herself that she did what she could, and it was now time to cut her losses. She should think, at least, about saving her close family, even if she couldn't save her entire people.

A DEBT REPAID

But Esther does not take this path. Instead, she chooses to risk her life – and to reciprocate a centuries-old act of selfless kindness.

Judah had once promised Jacob that he would guarantee the safety of Benjamin, come what may. But Judah never suspected how harshly destiny would call upon him to back up every inch of that promise. How tempted must Judah have been simply to give up and go home when Benjamin was found with the Egyptian's silver goblet in his sack. Yes, he had pledged to safeguard Benjamin, but what was he supposed to do now? No one asked Benjamin to steal the cup! Judah easily could have reasoned that it was time to cut his losses, time to give up on Rachel's child Benjamin and save his full-blooded brothers, the other children of Leah.

But Judah didn't do that. He made a direct appeal to the Egyptian to save Benjamin – and put his own safety in jeopardy to do it. Yes, there had been a time when Judah had abandoned the child of a rival mother, when he had allowed a child of Rachel to languish in slavery while he and the other brothers went home to their bereaved father. But it would not happen again. This time, Judah[2] would willingly become the slave so that a child of Rachel could go free:

> How can I possibly go back to my father without the lad? How can I possibly bear to see the terrible [fate] that will befall my father?

---

2. We noted above that almost all the names of the children of Leah and Rachel reflect a note of anguish or longing for Jacob's love. A notable exception to this is the name of Judah. It comes from the word "thanks": Leah had said, upon his birth, "This time I will thank God" (Gen. 29:35). In Hebrew, the root for *lehodot,* "to thank," has a double meaning; it also means "to admit." The common thread in these two ideas, thanks and admission, is the idea of unflinching recognition of uncomfortable truths: When one thanks another, he is acknowledging a certain indebtedness that he has to the other, a certain imbalance in the relationship. I might like to think we are on equal footing, but in truth, you have done me a kindness, and I am in your debt. Similarly, when one admits he's wronged another, he also recognizes a certain imbalance, a certain indebtedness he has to the other. For this reason, expressions of apology and of thanks can sometimes be the hardest words to say.

   In his speech to Joseph, Judah comes face-to-face with highly uncomfortable truths, and in so doing, makes one of the hardest recognitions of all: he cannot change the way his father feels about his family, and he must accept that rather than struggle against it. His earlier attempt to "set things right" by ridding the family of an inconvenient child of Rachel was ill-advised, to say the least. Now that he has the chance to relive that scenario, he will do things differently. Judah – a man named for an uncomfortable recognition – not only creates a hope of bridging the divide in his family, he also actualizes a certain potential inherent in his own name.

When did Benjamin ever repay Judah for those heroic words? It took centuries, but the answer is right now, right here in the Megilla. Judah was safe, but traded his own safety for the life of Benjamin, a child from the other side of the family. And now, centuries later, Esther, a descendant of Benjamin, is safe. But she sacrifices that safety so that the Judahites, from the other side of the family, might have a chance at survival. In so doing, Esther knows the historical significance of her actions. And she rightfully echoes Judah, the man whose kindness she now repays:

> How can I possibly bear to see the destruction of my kin? How can I possibly bear to see the terrible [fate] that will befall my people?

A HIDDEN STORY OF FAMILY RECONCILIATION

With seven heartfelt words, Judah did more than he could possibly imagine to bring together the bitterly divided sides of a grieving family. If only for a moment in time, the family was whole again; the terrible breach between the children of two mothers had been salved.

Over time, that rivalry between the children of Leah and the children of Rachel would continue to express itself. Ages later, rival kings would lead the two halves of the family, and the bitter divide would reassert itself. But here, at the close of the Bible, in the Megilla, is a ray of hope. Judah's healing words once again find an echo. Esther risks all for the children of Leah, and Judah's heroic act is knowingly reciprocated. The long arc of a circle has finally been closed.

MORDECAI'S POLL NUMBERS

As we noted earlier, the Megilla ends on a curious note. Its very last verse tells us that Mordecai, second in charge to the king, was good to his compatriots, that most of his brethren liked him, and that he sought their welfare and their peace:

> For Mordecai the Jew was second in charge to Ahasuerus; he was great among the Jews, and pleasing to most of his brethren; he sought the welfare of his nation, and spoke words of peace to all his children. (Est. 10:3)

It seems a strange way to end the Megilla. Instead of saying something about how God's hidden miracle was finally complete, how the heroics of a few good people saved the entire Jewish people, or something else suitably inspiring, the Megilla talks about Mordecai's successful political career and, strangely enough, his poll numbers. We learn that most but not all of his brethren kind of liked Mordecai. Why is this, of all things, the best way to end the Megilla's epic story?

In light of all that we've seen, the meaning of the verse – and its suitability as a way to close the Megilla – can now be apprehended. Read the verse again – but this time, everywhere the verse seems to mention "Jews," substitute the more nuanced Hebrew word *Yehudi*. Recall that *Yehudi* doesn't really mean Jew; it means a Judahite, someone from the Kingdom of Judah. The poignancy of the verse now shines through…

Mordecai, from the Kingdom of Judah, rose to a position in power. For most of Jewish history, the tribe of Benjamin was a mere footnote, an ancillary part of the Kingdom of Judah. But now a man from Benjamin would rise to the forefront and represent the remnants of Judah's kingdom. He would become the second-most-powerful man in the world.

Given the history of strife between the two sides of the Jewish family, the great question that fate would ask is: How did Mordecai acquit himself when it came to the rest of the Jewish family? How did he relate to them, and how did they relate to him?

Not everyone liked him. Not everyone from Judah could be expected to like being ruled by a Benjamite. But most found him pleasing. And as for him? He sought their welfare and spoke peacefully to all his children.

That last phrase, the part about "speaking peacefully" (in Hebrew, *dover shalom*) to all his children – that is, to all the people – what are we to make of it? We've heard those words before, too; any idea when the Bible first uses this phrase?[3]

It was in the Book of Genesis,[4] in a story that's now all too familiar:

> [And the brothers of Joseph] hated him, and could not speak peacefully to him. (Gen. 37:4)

The great schism in the family of Israel began when Joseph – a child of Rachel – was his father's deputy, and the children of Leah resented him so much that they could not speak in peace to him. It ends when a child of Rachel is once again deputy – this time, second in charge to the emperor of the civilized world – but this time, peace is spoken. Mordecai chooses to "speak peace" to the other side of the family. Loved by some – but not all – of them, he could have been kind to his friends and eliminated his enemies. But he makes a different choice. This time, there is no "other" side of the family. As the last words of the Megilla tell us, this time, they are all his children.

> And he spoke peacefully to all his children. (Est. 10:3)

THE LONG VIEW

In the end, Mordecai and Esther are heroes – not just because they maneuvered cleverly in difficult circumstances, and not just because they placed their faith in God when the chips were down.

---

3. My thanks to Avi Sussman, who brought this parallelism to my attention.
4. The first time the phrase appears in the Bible is in the context of Joseph and his brothers, in the verse cited above, when the brothers can't speak peacefully to Joseph. The final time in the Bible where we hear of someone "speaking peacefully" to someone else is right here, in the Megilla, with Mordecai.

They did, but they did something else, too. They did what they could to heal a terrible divide in the Jewish family.

Esther understood that the events in which she participated were not just about Jewish survival in a particular, localized slice of time. Yes, Haman threatened the Jews; but for all the urgency of that threat, the real meaning of Esther's actions transcended her own narrow moment in history. She understood that she was a participant in a dance, a historical drama spanning centuries. A family conflict had torn away at the fabric of Jewish unity for generations. To truly succeed, Esther would need to respond not just to a momentary threat from an external foe, but to an age-old rift that threatened to tear apart her people from the inside. Her greatness is that she responded, effectively and compassionately, to both.

Esther reached back through the centuries to touch – and redeem – a moment from the dawn of Jewish history. As the years passed, her victory over external enemies would accrue more fame than her internal triumph did. Indeed, in our day and age, everyone knows how Esther saved us from Haman's leering minions; few remember how she saved us from other, self-inflicted wounds. But private victories are not necessarily less significant than public ones. And as we, Esther's descendants, seek to emulate her in our own lives, we would do well to remember that we honor her legacy not just in how effectively we battle the antisemites from the ramparts, but in how valiantly we sow peace amongst ourselves in our private domains, within our cities and within our homes.

Epilogue

Every Saga Has a Beginning

If we stand back and survey the Megilla as we have now come to see it, we find ourselves confronted with a document whose narrative arc is more expansive than we might have supposed. The Megilla, it turns out, is not just a story of political intrigue, or even a treatise on how God operates behind the scenes in history, working hidden miracles in everyday events. It may be all that, but it is more, too: it is a story about a family, about *our* family. It is a redemptive chapter in a dance – sometimes sweet, often bitter – between two sides of the family of Israel, the children of Rachel and the children of Leah. If we view the Megilla this way, its message is not just political, or even theological; it's personal. It is a story about us, the community of Israel – about ancient wounds that have torn us apart, and about ways we've healed, and still can heal, those wounds. It is a story about family – *our* family – about what pitfalls we must avoid, and what opportunities we must seize. It is a story whose lessons matter in a very practical, visceral way.

There's only one problem with reading the Megilla this way: to truly understand its import, we need to look beyond the book of Esther itself. Reading the Megilla on its own is like flipping open a book and reading nothing but its last few pages. The ending seems climactic, but a true understanding of its power and import demands perusal of the other chapters. The same applies here. To truly understand the actions of Esther, this queen we thought we knew, we need to go back and read the other chapters. We need to look at the stories in the Torah that set the table, as it were, for the Megilla.

To do that, we need to go beyond the connections we've seen thus far between Esther and Mordecai, Benjamin and Judah, and ask: What's the *rest* of the picture here? We need to go back to the beginnings of the schism that emerged in the House of Jacob, and trace the path of that schism through the various books of Tanakh. If we do our job well, we will find a hidden story that wends its way throughout biblical history, culminating in the book of Esther, and casting a bold and tantalizing new light on the Megilla's message.

In a forthcoming sequel to this book, we shall attempt to do just that. We shall go back to the early moments of the divide in the House of Jacob, and trace the threads of these narratives throughout Tanakh until we arrive, once more, at the Megilla. To start you thinking about that journey, though, allow me to leave you with a question to ponder.

SILENCE IN THE FAMILY

We saw earlier how Mordecai told Esther that if she chose not to go to the king and instead remained silent, she would be destroyed. We explained earlier why her silence would be so disastrous; like it or not, silence would make her complicit in the decree against the Jews. But Mordecai also told her something else. He told her that silence would destroy not just Esther herself, but someone or something else, too:

> If you remain silent at this time, you and your father's house will be destroyed. (Est. 4:14)

Mordecai makes an oblique reference to Esther's "father's house." What does he mean by this? A rather pedestrian possibility is that he is referring to Esther's relatives – aunts, cousins, uncles – in short, the rest of her family. While that's certainly possible, "father's house" seems to have a different connotation. It suggests the idea of legacy, of Esther's forebears, her ancestors. Mordecai seems to be suggesting that Esther's silence will doom not just her, but also those who came before her – her ancestors, whose legacy she is bound to uphold. But who, or what, would he mean by this? Our conviction that Mordecai is referring obliquely to an earlier time is heightened by something else about his statement:

> If you remain silent at this time, you and your father's house will be destroyed.

Why does he add that qualifier, "at this time"? The words seem superfluous. Obviously, he wants her to go to the king *right now*; when else would he want her to go? Once again, Mordecai seems to be alluding to the past. Esther must not remain silent *at this time*. Were she to do so, disaster might ensue, the same kind of disaster that apparently occurred *some other time*, sometime in the past.

But when? What "other time" is he talking about?

We noted earlier that there is more than one Hebrew word for silence. If we trace the one Mordecai uses to denote Esther's silence, *lehaḥarish*, we'll find that this word has a long and storied history in the Bible. And the very first time this word ever appears in Tanakh, it portends disaster.

There was a time, long ago, when someone in Esther's "father's house" remained silent, and the results were catastrophic.

Mordecai seems to be saying that, for the sake of her father's house, her ancestor's legacy, she cannot allow that to happen again.

When was that time – and why did that one fateful episode of silence continue to echo for generations in the Jewish family? It is a question worth exploring. Its answer will launch us on a fascinating journey through some of the most intriguing and difficult stories of the Bible, including the rape of Dinah, the concubine in Gibeah, Saul's ascent to the throne of Israel, and David's battle against Goliath. But all that is more than we have time for now. It will have to wait for another book – one that will hopefully appear, not too long from now, in a Purim season yet to come.

The fonts used in this book are from the Arno family

Also by Rabbi Fohrman:

The Beast That Crouches at the Door

The Exodus You Almost Passed Over

For video courses related to the Purim story and the other topics discussed in this book, check out www.alephbeta.org

Maggid Books
The best of contemporary Jewish thought from Koren Publishers Jerusalem Ltd.